61 Minutes
Reflections and Homilies from the Year of Mark

by
Rev. Michael W. Rothan

authorHOUSE®

AuthorHouse™
1663 Liberty Drive, Suite 200
Bloomington, IN 47403
www.authorhouse.com
Phone: 1-800-839-8640

First published by AuthorHouse 11/14/2008

ISBN: 978-1-4389-1414-5 (sc)

Printed in the United States of America
Bloomington, Indiana

This book is printed on acid-free paper.

Contents

For my family.
Who is the most visible sign
of God's love for me,
in the world.

FOREWORD

Listen…

Is the first word in the rule of Saint Benedict. Benedict the Abbot was born around 480 and is considered the Father of Western Monasticism. His followers were mostly lay people who wanted to grow in relationship with God by banding together under a rule of life.

In this rule he advises his followers to *listen with the ear of the heart*. We spend so much time talking, even in our prayer, that we miss the Voice of God prompting us to live a fuller, happier life.

If there is any place where the Lord speaks to us and where we need to listen, it is at the Celebration of the Eucharist – The Mass. The Liturgy of the Word at every Mass necessitates a reflective prayerful listening to the Sacred Readings. All too often the Lord speaks to us through the Sacred Text, but we have no time to listen. The Liturgy has moved on to the next phase.

While this is true with the readings it is also true with the homily. The Lord might speak to us a personal word of comfort or challenge in the homily, but we are unable to prayerfully listen to that word, because the homily has moved on to the next thought.

Father Michael Rothan is a gifted homilist, who has inspired many by his insightful, reflective and enthusiastic homilies at Sunday Masses. Many people, over the years, have asked for a copy of his homily so that they might experience it again in a more personally reflective way. They wanted to listen with the ear of the heart to what the Lord was saying to them.

Their promptings has produced this set of homilies based on the Sunday Readings for Cycle B, the year of St. Mark.

I encourage you to read first the sacred text referenced at the beginning of each homily, and then slowly and prayerfully read through the homily stopping often to listen to the voice of the Lord with the ear of your heart to experience a personal word of comfort, challenge or insight.

Rev. Msgr. William M. Richardson
Pastor, Sacred Heart Church, Lewisburg, PA

July 11, 2008 – the Feast of Saint Benedict

INTRODUCTION

Stop and read this first! No, really. So often we experience life without the benefit of reflection. It is only when we are sick, or injured and are "forced" to slow down that we do. But even then we are sometimes so angry or depressed about having to slow down, that we don't think to use the time as a sort of retreat; or at worse, we are spiteful and refuse to use it, thinking it simply a waste of time. The truth of the matter is, we live in a world that judges us based on what we can produce. Therefore, when it comes to prayer; a diary; reflection; things we do alone, or perhaps do, knowing that others will never see or experience them, we see them as a waste of time. We perceive these practices as something "lame" or things that don't really fulfil a purpose at all.

This is what theologians and psychologists alike would call "bull-crap!" The fact is that so often we don't invest ourselves in prayer because it's not productive. Fr. Peter van Breeman says: "Resist the inclination to make prayer productive."[1] Very true! There will be no paper product or project; there is no certificate or degree that goes with it. However, what does come (eventually, as with anything else this takes time) is a *peace*. It is not a peace that denies that evil exists; nor is it one that is devoid of suffering. But it is a peace that enables simple *lived* experience to grow into the fullness of meaning. Our experiences are merely a page in the book of history unless we find meaning in them. If we can do that, then even the most painful experiences can bear fruit that will help us to become the people we were created to be.

Each of us is given the gift of imagination. Many of us don't tap into this gift; what a loss! Because it's the everyday stuff that not even our imagination can conjure up; and yet imagination can help us to unlock the secrets that God has subtly hidden in our everyday lives. I'll admit I was a skeptic at first as well. But look, I tried this and promised to do it for thirty days. For thirty days I would look over my day and write down stuff that happened during the day: seemingly boring stuff, and just everyday stuff. I figured, thirty days is thirty days. After that time if I haven't changed then I haven't lost anything. But if I *have* changed....wow. And so here I am, and here it is. Sometimes, I've found that the best way to teach is to show how. We are the best witnesses when we live what we teach. For this reason, I've compiled my reflections and homilies for the Sundays and major Holy Days throughout the year.

The title of this book is "61 minutes". We are all called, as priests, to make a holy hour, or spend 60 minutes in front of the Blessed Sacrament; in the presence of God each day. I would find myself praying for maybe fifty minutes and I would receive nothing in the way of inspiring thoughts or insights. Because I wasn't getting anything, I would be tempted to leave early. But if I stayed, I found over time that it was usually the fifty-eighth or fifty-ninth minute that God chose to enlighten me. I had to be faithful. Is it any wonder that Jesus asked the apostles in the garden to stay awake with him and pray? So now, just to make sure I give God all the time He needs, I make my holy hour 61 minutes. Just in case!

I had always written homilies in long-hand on a legal pad. Sometimes using shorthand or symbols; cues, etc. There came a time when one of my parishioners was stationed in Iraq fighting the war, so I began to send some homilies to him to make him feel "not so far from home." I began to compile, never with the intention to publish. After many arguments and justifications by those who wanted something to hold onto, however, I decided to relent. The title of the book gives credit where the credit is due. These thoughts and reflections, although written with my hand, are the work of the Holy Spirit. They are in fact physical products of a holy hour, so I give the glory to God.

Now here's the disclaimer part. First of all, these are homilies and homilies are meant to be heard, not so much read. Therefore, I have written these reflections the way they would be spoken. That being said, you will find sentence fragments; prepositions that end sentences; commas everywhere; bold and italics when necessary. I do this so that you might read it in the way that you would have heard it preached.

Second *caveat*, I read many books, and when I hear something that touches my heart personally, or something that will help me to explain something better, I use it. "A good homilist is an excellent thief," sayeth Fulton Sheen. What happens, however, is after awhile these things become your own. You can't remember where you read them or heard them. Within this writing, I've tried to give the original author credit if I used their quote or idea. But some I either couldn't find, or couldn't remember. So, if I used your quote, let me know and I'll give you credit in future editions. I encourage you (as I was encouraged in seminary) to read the readings for Sunday on your own first. Do this about ten times and I guarantee you, the meaning will change for you over time. Keep a light journal of significant experiences throughout the day and week. Put the scripture and your journal together and God will speak. After that…you can peek in here and see what came to me. Enjoy! Read, Re-Read, underline and teach!

Rev. Michael W. Rothan
Written at hermitage *Pangaea*

7 July 2008

---

1 *Fr. Peter van Breeman, SJ., The God Who Won't Let Go, (Notre Dame, IN: Ave Maria Press, 1991), 12.*

FIRST SUNDAY OF ADVENT
(CYCLE B)
(ISAIAH 63:16B-17, 19B; 64:2-7; 1 CORINTHIANS 1: 3-9; MARK 13:33-37)

Time to wake from sleep.

I ran around all day the last few days trying to find candles for our Advent wreathe. I finally ended up getting these *aroma-therapy* candles at two different stores. But here's the irony. Why did I have to look so hard?! These stores have had their decorations up for Christmas since October, and when I ask them about Advent, they have no clue. They know plenty about that special gift for *him* or *her*, but not about our Lord's coming. They have no clue.

As if that's not enough, I was charging through the malls looking for these things, and this girl approaches me to try and sell me some hand cream or something for my wife. I told her I wasn't married so she said, "Then for your girlfriend." I told her I didn't have one. I said, "I'm a priest, I won't ever be married," and she turned a bit red and said, "Oh I'm so sorry." Welcome to my world! As I experienced this girl at the kiosk and the various sales people at the candle shops, two words came to me again and again...WAKE UP!!

This *needs* to be said. How many of you have ever been driving to a destination (in either a car, or even on a bike for kids) and you remember leaving...and remember arriving...but the in-between. It's like a forgotten dream. How many of you have experienced this? (people raise their hands...and quite a few *did* as you can imagine) This is SCARY! What's wrong with people? Where are our minds? But think...some people go through life this way. True...how do I know?

People have often approached me and said: "You have so many stories and experiences for someone so young. How is that?" My response is always the same. I don't believe I have any more stories or experiences than anyone else. What I DO have, is an examined life. To find meaning in even the smallest moments; to reflect on them and share them with others in a way that might help them to grow. An unexamined life, is a life unlived.

I realize doing the same thing can become monotonous. I was concerned about this when I became a priest, knowing that some days I might celebrate Mass three times (God forbid it). Then I considered that this is for the rest of my life. And yet the Lord has offered me the grace to make it real...every time. I have to smile when I come up at the entrance and kiss the altar because it's like coming home....every time. Some people will live life as though there will always be time later to enjoy the scenery...there will always be time to get their life in order. We live like we can glide through now without a thought of tomorrow. WAKE UP! Because the Lord is coming....like a thief in the night he comes....will you be ready?

Second Sunday of Advent
(Cycle B)
(Isaiah 40:1-5, 9-11; 2 Peter 3:8-14; Mark 1:1-8)

If this were my last day, what could I say about my life?

"Prepare the way of the Lord. Make straight his path." Here is a guy out in the desert telling us to make a *way* for the Lord. When you think about it though, why would the Lord need a way paved for *Him*. I mean, let's face it…when He comes back in His glory, He won't be waiting for a road. He's gonna come in glory and majesty and so will get here regardless. So what could the prophet be saying during this time of anxious waiting? Make a way…a straight way?

What if the Lord returned right at this moment? What if He returned today right now? Some might miss Him if He returned here, because they won't be at church today, but if He returned to the place where you were this day. What would be His concern do you think? What would He want to know?

Do you think He'll care about the championship trophy you won in 1985, or whether you were MVP for your team? Or will He not be more concerned with how you entered into the *contests of brotherly opposition*; how you worked with your team toward a goal.

Do you think He'll ask about your promotion, or position in the company; the summer home or the big salary? The cars or the vacations? Or will He not ask about how much time you spent with the family He gave you. Whether you played with your children or taught them the ways of the faith. Or perhaps do you think He'll be concerned about how many degrees you earned, how many movies you starred in or the number of magazines you adorned with your body? Or will He not ask how many people you drew closer to Him through the gifts He entrusted to you; how many you led to Him through your example? Or maybe will He ask how many toys you bought your children or how you indulged them and allowed them to be free

8

in their choices of entertainment; how many friends they had or how much free time they were given. Or, more than likely, He would ask how did you train them in the ways of the faith, to love ME above all else in the world. Did you give them the faith?

The *way* that the prophet speaks of is not a road or a highway. The way that needs to be prepared for Christ…is a *way of life*! A way of life that leads to Him. Because be aware, that He *IS* returning…like a thief in the night. And on that day his concern will be the WAY you have paved with your very life!

Third Sunday of Advent
(Cycle B)
(Isaiah 61:1-2a, 10-11; 1 Thessalonians 5:16-24;
John 1:6-8, 19-28)

We cannot give what we do not have; we must know the faith!

John is a voice crying out in the wilderness. But there were many people crying out in the desert back in his time…why did so many come to listen to *him*? Why was it that even kings, who cared nothing for goodness or truth were moved by *him*? What was it he was to preach? Let's look at Isaiah and there, the message seems obvious. We are to preach the *GOOD NEWS*! This is a wonderful command. How often we have good news and we're just dying to call someone and share it. Amidst the crises in the world it can be discouraging and we might be tempted to give up hope. That is why this Sunday in Advent is so important…it gives us hope.

But if **we** are to be the voice crying out…a voice that people are going to listen to…one that brings good news, then we must *know the faith*! We cannot give what we do not have. And to know the faith means more than simple memorization; it means more than a knowledge of scriptural passages (even historians know as much). It means making our faith a part of us. It means realizing what a treasure we have in our Sacred Deposit of Faith and wanting to share that with others.

I bring this up because I saw a fantastic movie on Friday. In fact I would be willing to extend the offer, that if you went and saw it and didn't like it, I would give you your money back. However, I know none of you would take me up on that offer, and so I won't promise that. The movie was well made and the special effects outstanding, but what made this movie so special; what made it come alive was the treasure of our Church and our Sacred Deposit of Faith. The movie was *The Lion the Witch and the Wardrobe*.

I'm embarrassed to say that I never read those books (since then I have read the entire series). I read Lewis' *Great Divorce*; the *Four Loves, Mere Christianity, The Screwtape Letters, A Grief Observed*, among others, but not his *Chronicles of Narnia*. It was all I could do to keep from turning around, time after time and saying: "Do you people know what's going on here? Do you know who these characters represent?!" I thought how sad that many will attend such an event and reduce it to simple mythology or special effects when there are truths that appear throughout. So what do you need in order to make this movie real? Knowledge of the Faith and *Sacramental Imagination*.

Without giving the movie away, you should know: Jesus is the lamb of God, who is known as the Lion of Judah. He had a humble beginning and was called upon because Man in the beginning had sinned and with that sin the gates of heaven would be closed forever. Because of that all that gave life was absent from the earth and the devil was allowed to reign. Only God can breath his Spirit, his life into those whose sins have frozen them in darkness. You should know that Jesus chose followers from the normalcy of life. Of these followers, one would betray him, one would deny him and the rest would desert him at his hour of need. That he would give of his own blood that would have the power to heal. That in giving his own life he would destroy death and evil forever. That Evil is always ugly and any beauty it promises is simply a lie. That Peter was the rock on which he built his Church, that in Nathaniel there was no guile and even the betrayer could be forgiven. You should know that good will triumph over evil in the end, even when that evil seems to have won. That suffering and death, when offered for another, become redemptive, and that a Lion a witch and a wardrobe can become a reality, when you know the faith you have been given.

See, today many people are selling their own brand of theology and market it as fiction. There is a series called "Left Behind" which is a strong medium for selling anti-Catholicism. There was the "*Da Vinci Code*" from a few years ago which is still stirring the minds of people. What is happening, is that people are selling theology (and becoming rich) off of fear, and sharing their own brand of "faith." When people read this fiction, however, they are accepting it as fact. Therein lies the danger.

We must know the faith if we are to take it to the corners of the earth. We must love our faith and traditions which have become a part of life and if we do, it will become our life, not just some accessory added on to the other things. We are called to be the voices crying out in the wilderness; this will require that we know our faith enough to carry it out. Take advantage of any opportunities you can. Read whatever you can and if you have doubts, look for an *imprimatur* or ask someone who knows. If we embrace our Catholic Christian faith for the wonderful *sacred deposit* it is; if we believe what our Church teaches to be true, then a movie can become much more than simple fantasy or mythology…it becomes a voice of truth in the world. Even a world *that knows not the Christ.*

FOURTH SUNDAY OF ADVENT
(CYCLE B)
(2 SAMUEL 7:1-5, 8B-12, 14A, 16; ROMANS 16:25-27; LUKE 1:26-38)

What kind of house will you build for Me?

The Lord tells Nathan: "Go, tell my servant David, 'Thus says the Lord: Should you build me a house to dwell in?'" In other words, "What kind of house could you possibly build for me?" It's ironic that the Lord would pose such a question, because it is He who build the house that is David. You see, in the ancient world, the heart, was called the *domus*, or house. That's where we get the word *ab-domen* (away from the house, literally). So God created the heart of David...gave him the foundation with which to work, but it was up to David to finish the product.

That's why the question of God is so profound. What kind of house will you build for me? It's obvious that throughout his lifetime, David built a house that at times would not protect life within it, nor would it keep bad elements from without. A house that was built and torn down, rebuilt, and torn down time and time again. The faulty craftsmanship was a result of not working with the divine carpenter.

Contrast David, with Mary. The angel greets her as "full of grace." Grace the presence of God within us, and Mary is filled with that presence. No room for anything else. Her house had been built for our Lord and was structured in such a way that she became the Ark... the new Eve. The entry of God into her house would be harkened by one word... "*Fiat*" or "Be it done!" This "yes" would echo throughout her life. As the house continued to grow in depth and strength through suffering and sacrifice she would welcome others into her house. Again, the Lord would ask her to make a place as he offered John his mother, and his mother John.

The Lord has created us to journey through this life, but never alone. He has called us, much as He called Mary, to welcome our Lord; that we might receive His Word so completely that it becomes incarnate in us. That we might be that house.

Christmas Homily
(Cycle ABC)
(Isaiah 9: 1-6; Titus 2:11-14; Luke 2: 1-14)

Openness is the necessary disposition to receive a gift.

There is a Christmas story I guarantee you haven't heard yet. This is not one that will be on the television stations, or in the theatres…it's much too subtle for that.

The man, and the woman with child, slowly walked along the narrow city streets of Bethlehem. They had traveled very far and didn't stop through the nights. It was now nightfall and the woman was tired and sick. She was well into her last days of pregnancy and had been riding on a donkey for days. The man spotted an inn off the road, and hoped for the best. He knocked heavily on the solid door, but no one stirred inside. He looked back at his wife, now sweating and labored, and he pounded on the door again, unwilling to accept rejection. Again there was no sound from within. Finally, after offering a silent prayer he knocked a third time. There was some sound from within, and suddenly a little square slot slid open at the top of the door and a man's face filled the opening.

"What do you want? It's late."
The man replied: "Please, we need a place to stay. We're so tired and have traveled many miles."
The innkeeper replied, "I'm tired as well! Many people have traveled to get here, but there's no room. I'm sorry." And he went to shut the little slot but the man stayed it with his hand.
"Please…my wife is about to give birth to our first born. We will sleep on the floor, in the window, wherever, we just need a place. Even if you can only take her…please."
The innkeeper was becoming irritated and yet he did feel pity. (Was that the first time he's felt pity in years?…)
"Fine. There's a barn up on the hill. There's an ox there, a donkey

and some geese. You can stay there. But don't light any lamps or fires....that's all I need is for the whole barn to go up!"

The man was most grateful, and he and his wife journeyed to the top of the hill and to their resting place. Meanwhile, the innkeeper was angry. "Why does everyone depend on me for stuff? Why do MY feelings not matter? I'm always doing for everyone else...I work the day away and for what? My family never sees me; my friends don't know me anymore. I've fallen away from my faith... from those who love me; I've fallen away from my family. And you God....I've waited for so long for you to do something, and you do nothing! I ask for very little and yet you never answer my prayers." He went to bed, and the last words he spoke before sleep overtook him were these: "How I've waited for you to enter my life, my world, and you never so much as knocked at the door".... then he thought.

He dreamt about his life and where it was going. He was a young father and husband and yet saw that he was essentially living to work, and not working to live. Then he thought about that poor woman about to give birth. He got up from bed and his wife asked: "Simon, where are you going?" But he left the house without a word. He wanted to check on the couple. He put on his robe and walked out into the cool night air. He could hear the crickets chirping and the wind rustling through the olive grove. He heard the brook flowing along the path and the waterfall up ahead. He looked up at the barn and saw it was dark. They were probably freezing tonight. And then, something amazing happened.

All at once the world stilled. The leaves were silent, and the water froze in its path. The creatures paused their chatter and all the world was still, as in awe of some great event. And then, just as suddenly the world moved again. The creatures continued to stir and the water flowed and the breeze blew, and now looking up at the barn he saw light.

"I told them not to light a lamp!" He scowled, and now doubled his pace to get to the barn. As he approached he heard sheep (he didn't have any sheep) and he saw a crowd around the barn. He made up his mind to throw them out. See how people repay you for generosity! He got to the barn and the words rising sharply to his lips were at once stifled as his eyes feasted on a timeless moment. He was dumbfounded. A child, lay in his mother's arms and light seemed to be coming from everywhere. There was no fire, but light. Then the child looked at him as though he recognized him from long ago. The innkeeper was so dumbfounded that he simply stood there gawking at the sight. A shepherd holding a lamb went over to him and said: "Hold this" and he was so struck he did it. (And to this day, it is actually the innkeeper holding the lamb in the manger scene and not a shepherd). The shepherd then got down on his knees in homage to the child. And the child's name was Jesus.

He saw the boy's father take one of his old troughs for feeding, which bore his brand burned into the wood, and put straw in it and used it for a bed for the child. Simon didn't remember how long he stood there, just watching. But he knew that *God* was *with him* that night… and his life was changed forever. He never thought of the little boy and the family again…until.

Thirty years later; since that night years before, he had made his family second only to God…the God who had knocked and asked for room….back then, there *was* no room. Now, Simon was in Jerusalem with his family to celebrate the Passover. And as he walked the streets there was a commotion. In an effort to see what was going on, he approached the crowd and was immediately pushed into the street by a Roman soldier. "Help the prisoner, he'll die before he reaches the hill." Simon pleaded that he wanted nothing to do with this, that he was with his family and continued on but the soldier cut him off and pushed him toward the condemned man. He lifted the wood, and as he did so his eyes caught a stray mark….a brand burned into the wood. This was once his manger. This wood….this cross belonged to him. And as Simon looked at the condemned man, the man looked up, and

Simon saw the child who saved his life so many years ago. The child who was cradled once by this wood, now cradled this wood; and then Simon the Cyrenian came to understand that he was in Jerusalem for God…as God came to Bethlehem for him.[2]

Sometimes we invite God into our lives, but there's no room. Sometimes we must go places where we don't want to be; sometimes we must carry things we'd rather not carry. Simon held a lamb outside a barn and was given life. He helped bear a cross, within a death march and was given salvation.

---

2 *My own original story, based on the Apocryphal Gospels.*

FEAST OF THE HOLY FAMILY
(CYCLE ABC)
(SIRACH 3:2-7, 12-14; COL. 3: 12-21; MATT. 2:13-15, 19-23)

The true treasure is right here.

Dr. Phil was once quoted as saying: "95% of all families are dysfunctional; the other 5% are in denial." I think that quote could be true, certainly for extended families. It depends on what *they* mean by dysfunctional. Dysfunctional means "an impairment of function" and yet many families that are categorized as "dysfunctional" continue to function quite well. Ask yourself is this sounds like a "dysfunctional family".

The girl, only fourteen at the oldest is pregnant; she's not married, but engaged to a very nice guy, who wants to take care of her. They are both poor. They marry despite the scandal that is caused by the rumors about them. By the time they have the child they are forced to move and so are homeless. The child must be born in a barn, surrounded by animals. They have no insurance or healthcare; no foodstamps or WIC. Once they settle in the area, however, they have to flee again because of political unrest and the threat of infanticide. They go to Egypt where they've never been, where they have no relatives and where there is no temple or synagogue, and live there for some time. When they return home, they no longer have a home, because *squatters* have moved in.

Now…if that's not a rough start, I don't know what is. By all practical standards, this would be a dysfunctional family. But today we celebrate the "Holy Family." How could one that started off so terribly wrong, be considered holy? Because Holy is not something we can do…it is something God does. Paul says to the Colossians: Put on, as God's chosen ones, holy and beloved, heartfelt compassion, kindness, humility, gentleness, and patience, bearing with one another and forgiving one another, if one has a grievance against another; as the Lord has forgiven you, so must you also do. And over all these put on love.

What distinguishes a *Holy* Family from the other, is not that it lacks disasters or problems, or that God prevents evils from occurring within it. What distinguishes a *Holy* Family is their Faithfulness and Love for each other despite, these difficulties. And this is where the treasure lies.

This story was one I received through an email that really seems to sum it up.

There was a man in his seventies, who had spent his whole life traveling the world. He was never pinned down by the worries or pains of a wife and family. He had so many adventures and stories to tell, but now in his late years, there was no one to tell them to. He was so grateful when he ran into a great nephew of his. This nephew had always appreciated his uncle and the many adventures he had experienced. So the nephew asked his uncle to come and live with his wife and children. The uncle was most grateful for this opportunity, because he would not be alone. The nephew would sit and listen to the stories of adventures and long to be his uncle. He often voiced that he could go no where and do nothing because he had to care for his family, but that he was living the adventures through his uncle. One evening as his uncle was telling of some faraway place he mentioned a map of buried treasure. The idea stuck in his nephew's head so that when his uncle died, the nephew went through all the man's belongings, and with shaking fingers and pounding heart, he found an envelope with his name. He opened the envelope and sure enough there was a map that pointed to the Treasure. This would surely change his life, a real treasure. The map began at a red barn out in the middle of nowhere, and so he drove out there, got out of the car and began to walk. He followed the map meticulously, making sure all of his steps were accurate. As he got further he realized that he was entering his own neighborhood, and joy filled his heart. He thought: "He must have buried it here, it's so close." Finally he pinpointed the last location…it was his home. His uncle had left him a treasure and at that moment, the nephew found it. The realization that his own home; his own family; was the treasure; and a priceless one indeed.[3]

Some might say the treasure beyond all price.

---

3 *Internet Forward.*

SOLEMNITY OF MARY
(CYCLE ABC)
(NUMBERS 6:22-27; GALATIANS 4:4-7; LUKE 2: 16-21)

Any good change takes time.

Why did the shepherds come to see Jesus? Think about this...set up the scene. The sky is dark, and here are these shepherds out in the middle of nowhere. They're bedding down for the night and one of them is keeping the watch. Suddenly a multitude of heavenly host fills the sky, and ring out "*Hosannas* in the highest!" You can imagine the sight...imagine the fright. They give them a prophecy and direction and then they depart. Now some might stand there and say, "Wow," while others were snapping pictures the whole time, and will never recall actually seeing the angels. But some...will have listened to what the angels said, and to see angels would not be enough...they wanted to see the Creator of the angels. THAT's why there are angels up here in the manger scene.

But they had to be looking for something more, or they would have stayed put. If they had been truly satisfied with their lives, they would have had no reason to go. Many people will say, "Before I die, I wanna see the world." These shepherds had only experienced a corner of the desert for most of their lives, and yet, they wanted to see the *Maker* of the world. That is sight. It is a searching for change, which is what this time of year is all about. A second chance. Why change? Is my life the way I want to live for the next seventy years? Am I ready to face my Creator this day?

If you have any doubts about the desire for change, just go to the "self help" section of the booksellers, and you'll see how many gurus are out there. From Oprah to Dr. Phil, from L. Ron Hubbard to Tony Little, they're all out there. There's a good story that was told by Rev. Anthony DeMello which demonstrates clearly how helpful these individuals can be, if you focus *only* on them and eliminate God from the equation.

There was a boy that was labeled "mildly retarded" by an evaluator. So they sent him to a special school. Johnny went to art modeling class for special children where he was given a piece of putty. He takes the little lump and goes to a corner of the room by himself and plays with it. The teacher comes up to him and says, "Hi Johnny." And Johnny says, "hi." The teacher says, "What's that you've got in your hand?" And Johnny says, "This is a lump of cow dung." The teacher asks, "What are you making out of it?" He says, "I'm making the teacher."

The teacher thought, "Poor little Johnny has regressed." So she calls out to the principal's office and says, "Johnny has regressed." So the principal who came by the classroom approaches Johnny and says, "Hi son." And Johnny says, "Hi." And the principal says, "What do you have in your hand?" And he says, "A lump of cow dung." "What are you making out of it?" the principal asked. And Johnny says, "The principal."

The principal thinks that this is a case for a *New Age* self-help Guru, and so sends for this sage. The self-help guy is a clever one, and he goes up and says, "Hi." And Johnny says, "Hi." And the Guru says, "I know what you've got in your hand." "What?" Johnny replies. "A lump of cow dung." Johnny says, "right." "And I know what you're making out of it." "What?" "You're making a counselor like me, right?" "Wrong," Johnny replied, "not enough cow dung!"......and they say he was retarded.[4]

We need to stop looking all around us for the answer that will be least painful for our lives. We need to stop thinking of the least uncomfortable way to change. We need to look at our fears, and step in that direction.

When I was younger, I entered a craft fair in grade school. I wanted to make a church out of sugar cubes. I found I could only glue one level of sugar cubes at a time, and then had to let them dry. I would then glue the next level, but it was taking hours and I was getting tired of the intermittent waiting. After I had five levels of cubes I just continued to glue without allowing the lower levels to dry until

I reached the top. I had finished in much less time than I would have, had I glued and waited. The day of the fair, I was most proud of my structure. But on the ride to school we hit a bump, and the steeple cracked; then the van took a sharp turn, and Jesus flew off the cross and the bells dropped, and then a few windows fell out. With each bump and turn the once beautiful structure continued to erode. By the time I finally arrived at school (in tears) there were only five levels left…the first five I had taken time to build and allowed the time to dry.

These self-helps that eliminate the faith factor are much like that building. The structure that stayed in tact was made from those things that took time, and hard work; those things that we struggle through… it was those which were done in the best way. Those that were built in the way they were supposed to be, remained.

Look at your life through this lens, and see the things that have crept in over the year, and years. See the things that we have done hastily and shoddily, and then look at the things that have lasted. Look at this year as another opportunity at life. That you can "live today as though you're already living for the second time, and about to do all the same things you did the first time around….but change".[5]

If you need a model for this, we needn't look far. Mary is the blessed mother, because her soul magnified the Lord. She looked in the face of fear and journeyed toward it. We ask her constant help, that like the shepherds we might not be satisfied with where we are….not satisfied with **how** we are, but see that which the world cannot provide; we journey not toward a star, but toward the Son.

---

[4] *Fr. Anthony DeMello, S.J. Awareness: The Perils and Opportunities of Reality. (New York: Doubleday, 1992, 13.*

[5] *My Paraphrasing of Viktor E. Frankl. Man's Search for Meaning. 3rd ed. (New York: Simon and Schuster, 1984). 114.*

EPIPHANY OF THE LORD
(CYCLE ABC)
(ISAIAH 60:1-6; EPHESIANS 3: 2-3A, 5-6;
MATTHEW 2:1-12)

The one gift God cannot provide for Himself.

Today we celebrate the Epiphany of the Lord. This is the appearance of the Lord to those we now call kings, who were the "*magi*" or wise astrologers of the time. As I reflected on the readings today, which speak of a *light to the nations* to appear, and the whole drama amidst a king who wants to kill Jesus, and those who wish to adore him; my eyes were brought back time and time again to the Nativity scene.

I sat here in the darkness with only the scene illuminated, and focused especially on the kings. Why would they come? I mean let's face it, if you're a king, you have it all. They must have had subjects and castles, all the treasure and security one could muster. They brought some of the most valuable objects of the time period. So why did they come? The fact that they journeyed to see a baby, is a reflection of their own life…their own discontentment with life. If not discontent, then why leave…why journey for something more?

As I continued to reflect on these kings, I peered closer at each one individually. The Kings originally were made to represent the "whole world" of the time. There was an African looking king an Asian looking one, and a European one. I looked at the one crouching who was clearly looking at the Christ child. I then saw the other (which resembles Will Smith…uncanny) and he is looking at the parents. Then there was the third. He appeared to be simply looking out into space. It was as if he was focusing on nothing at all…just a blank stare. What was *HE* thinking, I wanted to know? Now don't get me wrong, I know they're statues…but statues modeled on real persons.

Was he perhaps thinking of his kingdom left behind? Or maybe they overthrew his kingdom and he just happened to join these others on the road. Maybe he was pondering his last days there, or wondering what his children were up to. Or maybe…he just realized that at his feet was his Creator. And that the former way of life he knew, and thought he loved, he could never return to again. Having seen God, he would never be the same again. He was considering what precious gift he could offer this child, that the child could not himself produce. And it was then that I realized what he was looking at.

He was not merely looking out into space, but was actually focused on something. He was asking the question, "What gift could I bring, that God Himself could not provide?" The gift captured his gaze. The God who could make gold, frankincense and myrrh could not provide Himself with this gift, and yet it is the only gift He desired. It is the gift He cannot bring himself. What the king is looking at…that gift….is YOU.

SECOND SUNDAY IN TEMPUS PER ANNUM[6] (CYCLE B)
(1 SAMUEL 3:3B – 10, 19; 1 CORINTHIANS 6:13C –15A, 17-20; JOHN 1:35-42)

God has created us to do something that no one before us could do.

We celebrate a special week focusing on Vocations: that call from God to enter more deeply into a relationship with Him that empowers us to serve others and bring them closer to Christ. The first reading and the Gospel echo this in their selective stories.

Samuel, who was a gift to Hannah in her elder years, becomes an apprentice to Eli. That's the part of the story we hear, but we missed part one. Hannah was given a son (which means now she and her husband have an heir and someone to carry on the family name) and she in turn returns her son to God. There is no question. Some might say, "Hey, God has given you this son as a free gift, so encourage him to marry and have children so that your name is not forgotten." And yet we know, by this very reading, that his name was not nearly forgotten. That Samuel would hear the voice of God very clearly, but that it would take someone older and wiser to help him discern that call.

That is what *vocation* is all about. It is not we who call God, but He who calls us, as unworthy or unprepared, inept as we might feel. But it will be the parents, and the older and wiser ones around those who are called, who will help the discernment. For this reason, it must be an option. The vocation to the priesthood or religious life is something that must be spoken of as a real possibility. We don't have a shortage of vocations. To say that is to say that God doesn't know what He needs. What we *have* is a shortage of people willing to say **yes**, to what God is calling them to do. That is not to say we should force vocations either, for a person who is called to be married, and becomes a priest or religious will never be happy. It means encouraging the call that is already there, despite our weakness and inadequacies.

That is why the Gospel here is so important. Who did Jesus call? He called Peter, a fisherman, and foul-mouthed hot-head. Called James and John the sons of thunder, each worried about who will sit at the sides of Jesus...*kiss-ups* if you will. Judas who will eventually betray him because he is so politically charged. Thomas, who wasn't sure what he believed and was always asking for clarications from Jesus. Matthew a tax-collector who cheated people of their money. Nathaniel who said what was on his mind, despite how it might affect those around him. Two non-churched individuals who were Greeks, amidst others. These were the guys in formation for three years who the Holy Spirit would use to guide the Church in the years ahead!

Who are the ones becoming these apostles today and answering the call?

Dave. I met him my second year in seminary. He had a degree in Biology and with his parents owned a golf course. He drove a BMW motorcycle and traveled all over the country on it. Until he got the call. He and his parents sold the golf course, and he entered the seminary, surrendering his bike for a car and six years later is now a priest in the diocese of Youngstown OH...and riding a Honda Goldwing now.

Rich Holdorf. I met him my first year. Fifty years old and a Doctor of pharmacy. He owned a store down in Charlotte NC and worked for many years in this old town. He doubled as a deejay, and often, when a teacher would make a reference to a song, Rich would shout out "The Drifters, 1954" or whatever the reference. He gave up his store and career to be a *fisher of men*, and is studying to be a priest for the diocese of Wheeling-Charleston.

Joe Dougherty. Blue collar guy from Philadelphia who was tired of the hustle and bustle of Philly and gave up his job and moved to Port Allegheny in Pennsylvania. He bought a farm and raised cattle, horses, chickens and corn, having never done that before. He worked in a factory for extra income, but there was a longing in him. At the age of 42, he entered the seminary, and is now a priest for the Diocese of Erie.

A guy who was a science teacher and had a business articulating and selling animal skeletons all over the country. You can find his work at the Baltimore aquarium, Sea World, and the Museum of Natural History, NY as well as Reptiland. Still something missing in life. He entered the seminary and was ordained June 5, 2004. He is a priest in the diocese of Harrisburg. It's me.

These are the fishermen that the Lord has called, regardless of their background. I know there are some of you out there right now, and you are on the fence. GET OFF OF IT!!! There are some who are not here who are being called…some of them in the chapel right now. You are the ones the Lord has sent to them, like Eli, to encourage that vocation. Make this an option for them. Encourage their exploration of this life. I love my life! I can't imagine a greater way to live and thank God for the gift of my vocation. There is only one major thing that separates the apostles and the priests that I just mentioned from those of you who are thinking, and those who haven't yet considered this an option….the only difference is the sentence: Here I am! Speak Lord your servant is listening.

---

6 ***Tempus per Annum****: Latin meaning "Time through the Year" in other words "Ordinary Time".*

THIRD SUNDAY IN
TEMPUS PER ANNUM
(CYCLE B)
(JONAH 3: 1-5, 10; 1 CORINTHIANS 7: 29 – 31;
MARK 1:14 – 20)

God could've created the world without us in it…but He didn't; why?

Forty days more and Ninevah will be destroyed. Jonah speaks to the Ninevites. But not immediately. He wanted to do nothing. It was only because Jonah changed his attitude, that the Ninevites were saved. Paul says to the Corinthians, "I tell you brothers and sisters, the time is running out! For the world in its present form is passing away." Finally, Christ says, "The kingdom of God is at hand. Repent and believe in the Gospel." All of these messages seem to resound with a kind of gloom and doom, and yet within each is a message. The message is "ENOUGH!"

Enough of what? Enough of your murder of the innocence…. Enough! Let me share with you some statistics that were given to priests at a workshop offered by Helen Alvarez who works for the American Bishops. These statistics are from 2004, as the 2005 are not out yet.[7] In 2004, and this is in Pennsylvania:

There were 36,000 abortions

33% women ages 20 – 24
17% were those age 18 and 19
6.2 % were those 15 – 17
187 for those 14
52 for those 13
64 for those 12 and under

of abortions, 46% had one prior abortion

In PA there are 101 facilities that abort babies. PA does not require licensing, but that they are *registered*...whatever that means.

Enough! Is this not a problem? Think about it. If laws were passed tomorrow making it legal to kill a child two years and under, what would we do? If two year olds all over the country were being killed and dismembered; being allowed to die without normal means of life support, would this not be an issue? Would this not be THE issue?! So what is the problem? The problem is that the Church, which Christ brought into being is *Pro-Life* through and through. She would never consider violence against an innocent. So if the Church Christ created is Pro-Life, what is the problem?

The problem is the people making up the Church are not unequivocally pro-life. Before you gasp at this in disbelief ask yourself:

Do I support the Death Penalty here in the United States? If you do, then you are not Pro-Life.

Do I support the right of a person to end their life if they are in pain or suffering? If you do, then you are not Pro-life.

Do I abuse drugs or alcohol; have I allowed my children to use alcohol or drugs? If you have, then you are not pro-life.

Do I support a woman's right to choose whether or not to have an abortion? If you do, you are not pro-life.

Do I use contraceptives, and (God forbid) provided them for my children? If you do, then you are not pro-life.

This world has convinced us through its clever use of the term "freedom" that we can live life easier by getting rid of the problems we create ourselves. This term freedom creates a prison within which we rot and starve. Ask any woman who has had an abortion if it liberated her...if she felt more like a woman. Ask any man who has had an abortion, if he felt as though his "problem was solved" or if he didn't think about it every single day!

This is a world that does not care about its victims, whether the one killed or the one carrying the killed. Because of this, the world will continue to claim its victims and yet has the audacity to curse God and say: "Where are the cures for these diseases you gave us? Where is the food for the hungry? Why do so many people suffer the ills of this world," and God will reply with the same question, but changed slightly.

"What did you do with the one I sent who was to cure cancer? Where is the soul I created who would eradicate poverty? Where is that one I made who would cure the disease?" And we will have to answer, we killed them. We killed our salvation, and yet why should this surprise us. Killing those sent to save us is not foreign to us...we started with the prophets, continued with the Christ and on throughout our own time, again and again.

And if you wonder whether or not you've been infected by this world's idea of freedom, ask yourself if you were offended by anything that was said today. If you were offended, then you've already been infected. But there is time. Even God stilled his hand with the Ninevites...even Paul gives us hope; but not without change. We change ourselves, and we can change the world. We stay the same, and the world gets worse. Jonah had to change his attitude first, only then was there a possibility that Ninevah would be saved.

---

7 *At the time this homily was preached, the statistics were not availible. Now in 2008, I'm sure there are more recent statistics. Check the Right to Life website for more information.*

Fourth Sunday in Tempus Per Annum (Cycle B)
(Deuteronomy 18: 15-20; 1 Corinthians 7:32-35; Mark 1:21-28)

We are called to be prophets

God could've made the world without you in it, but He didn't… why? God could've made the world without you in it, but He didn't why? He must have created you to do something that no one before you could ever do; and no one after you will ever be able to do. Something that is so special and so sacred, that when you fulfil this task for which He has created you different from any other, the world will be changed forever, because of you. That's the truth. That means you are completely unique! Look next to you and you are looking at the only one of their kind! (Resist the temptation to say thank God; but instead to *Thank* God!)

This is our vocation. A call from God, a unique purpose that will change the world forever. Doubt this for a minute? Then why didn't God create someone else. So what does this demand then? Other than absolute gratitude, (because this One who created you also gave you your first breath this morning,) we owe Him adherence to this purpose. First, we must recognize it, then live it. Moses knows this. Listen to him:

"A prophet like me will the Lord, your God, raise up for you from among your own kin." That's us he's talking about. And I would propose that some of the major prophets in our lives, we might not see; we might not hear because of what Paul calls: "anxiety about the things of the world." Those things can put a protective blinder over the eyes of our hearts. What does the Psalmist say, "If today you hear His voice (vocation) harden not your hearts." Where are these prophets then? They are among us…. Among our kin. We need only look.

I would like to introduce to you three of these prophets from my own life, who have had a profound impact on my priesthood: Mason, Sean, and Mandy.

My nephew Mason is now eight years old, but I recall when he was three, we used to play this game. It was a simple game to play. Mason would say, "Catch me, catch me, catch me......" and run at me, jump into my arms and I would catch him. Pretty simple right? But every now and then, I would be distracted or working on something, and I would hear this voice running up behind me, "Catch me, catch me catch me" and I would turn in just enough time, to see his body flying through the air....and then....bang! He would hit the floor. Usually that was about the time my sister would walk into the room and say: "What'd you do to my child?!" The irony, is that regardless of how many times I dropped Mason (it didn't happen that often....THAT often) he continued to run at me with absolute faith that I would catch him. That little prophet taught me what it meant to have faith...to really trust.

I am human, and there will be times when I will falter. There are times that we will fail those that we love most in the world...but God does not fail. Despite the times we may have felt as though He dropped us, sometimes, those instances are what we need to get on track again.

I was up north in Berwick, PA and it was the summer preceding my Diaconate ordination. I was working on comprehensive exams, independent study in Phenomenology, doing adult education amidst a plethora of other activities, and was probably burning out to an extent. I had lost focus of what I was supposed to be doing because of all the "stuff" I thought I had to do. At that moment, the Pastor asked me to take communion to a guy named "Sean." He was my age, and I was wondering why he wasn't coming to church.

Well, it turned out that Sean had cerebral palsy, so he was paralyzed from the chest down. His speech was slurred, but understandable. He had been bound to a wheelchair for most of his life and we had a nice chat, because we had a bit in common, despite his handicap. Towards the end of my visit, as I was planning to depart, Sean, out of the blue said: "You know, when I die I want to go to Heaven." I thought to myself, "Join the club, I wanna be there too some day." Then he looked up at me and said: "You know why I want to go to Heaven?" "Why Sean," I replied. "Because when I get to Heaven, I won't have this" and he slapped his legs; his legs that never ran; legs that never walked or played. And then he continued: "And you know what I'm gonna do when I get to Heaven? I'm gonna Dance! But I'm not gonna dance like the people here…you see they dance because they hear the music. No, when I get to Heaven, I'm gonna dance out of pure joy."

I left there that day, and I knew a prophet had been in my midst. And I went back to the Church and thanked God that my legs hurt, because it meant they worked. I thanked God that I was overworked with studies, because it meant I could have an education. Sean taught me that day, what it meant to hope. To hope is to see the best in every person and situation. I learned to hope that day.

I was a science teacher before entering the seminary and one such year I had a student named Mandy. Now Mandy was cantankerous. She had such a negative attitude about everything in life. My favorite time of day was homeroom because I would really get to know the kids. But often, Mandy would come up in homeroom and tell me about all the difficulties and problems she had in life…and then without batting an eye she would tell me that *I* was the source of most of those problems! Everything was *my* fault and she had no qualms about informing me of that daily. Finally she graduated from 8th grade and I left for seminary and we didn't communicate as did many student with me, over the next four years.

My final year in seminary I was struggling with the issue of change. I wondered after speaking to thousands of people who seemed "stuck" if people could change. I was really struggling with this question. Mandy's brother contacted me and said she was in the hospital and it seemed serious. I found myself on the way to the hospital to visit thinking: "What makes me think she would want any visitors, let alone ME the one who seemed to be the source of so many of her problems." As I entered the hospital room she was alone. She could neither speak nor open her eyes. I walked in and said: "Mandy, it's Mr. Rothan"…and she smiled.

Over the next month I visited her four other times and each time she improved. She now had her eyes open but still could not speak. I reflected that I was about to be ordained a deacon and yet during all these visits, not once did I offer to pray with her. Not once! I was worried that maybe she would say no, or do it begrudgingly, but this last time I was determined to pray. Her eyes were open this last visit, but she could not speak and as I entered the room the nurses said: "Don't touch her. We have wires and monitors and everything set up, so don't mess it up!" Finally as my visit was concluding I got up the courage and said: "Mandy, I would like to pray with you now, but the nurses said……." And she reached up and grabbed my hand. And I prayed the hardest prayer I ever prayed. I got up and kissed her on her head. And as I left that room I KNEW, PEOPLE CAN CHANGE! This awful girl had transformed through suffering into a loving woman from whom the words "I love you" rolled very easily from her lips in her final days. That was truly a gift. She taught me that people can change…that even those we think cannot possibly love, have the capacity.

The prophet speaks. That God will take care of us amidst our suffering and loneliness and pain. He is there to take care of us. These are the gifts God gives us daily, the subtle gifts that are often hidden in his minor prophets in life. The prophet is the one who has accepted the call…accepted the purpose our Lord has entrusted to them and struggles through life to proclaim that purpose to the world. When we can hear God's voice that clearly, and proclaim His message with conviction, then like Jesus, they will say of us: "This one is teaching with authority…that even the unclean spirits will obey."

Fifth Sunday in Tempus Per Annum
(Cycle B)
(Job 7:1-4, 6-7; 1 Corinthians 9:16-19, 22-23; Mark 1: 29-39)

What does it mean to be truly rich?

"In Some way, suffering ceases to be suffering at the moment it finds a meaning, such as the meaning of a sacrifice."[8] *Suffering breaks the illusion that we live in; the illusion that everything is okay. It breaks the illusion we live in and pares us down to what is most authentically human about us...our ability to love...even those people we don't even know.*

Listen to today's readings, and reflect on this:
A rich man's son was heading off to Law School and so the Father thought before he graduated college, he would take him on a trip. He decided to take him to a small town in Central America. He wanted to show his son a different culture, and although he was a little concerned because the area to which they were traveling was so poor, he thought it would be fun. They spent a couple of days and nights near farms of what would be considered very poor families. Over the next two weeks, the son grew very familiar with one of the families, from whom he learned much more than the language.

On their return from their trip, the father asked his son, "How was the trip?"

"It was great, Dad." And that was all they spoke of, until they returned home.

One day the son approached his father and made the announcement: "I'm not going to law school. I'm going to take my experience and education and go to where the poor are."

The father was stunned. "Son," he said, "please consider what you're doing."

"Did you see how poor people live?" the father asked.

"Oh yeah," said the son.

"I saw that we have one dog and they had four. We have a pool that reaches to the middle of our garden and they have a creek that has no end.

We have imported lanterns in our garden and they have the stars at night.

Our patio reaches to the front yard and they have the whole horizon.

We have a small piece of land to live on and they have fields that go beyond our sight.

We have servants who serve us, but they serve each other.

We buy our food, but they grow theirs.

We have walls around our property to protect us, they have friends to protect them." [9]

The boy's father was speechless. Then his son added, "Thanks, Dad, for the lesson. For showing me how poor **we** are."

There are types of poverty that go far beyond material things. "To be truly rich is not to have everything....but to need nothing."
--Mother Teresa

---

8 *Viktor E. Frankl. Man's Search for Meaning. 3rd ed. (New York: Simon and Schuster, 1984). 117.*

9 *Internet Forward*

Sixth Sunday,
Tempus per Annum
(Cycle B)
(Leviticus 13:1-2, 44-46; 1 Corinthians 10:31-11:1; Mark 1:40 – 45)

To be like Jesus means to perform miracles in our own lives.

Imagine what it would be like, if WE could perform miracles. What it would be like if we, like Jesus in the Gospel, had the power to not only take away a disease like leprosy, but restore a person to personhood. Imagine that power, to bring someone who was seemingly dead, back to life again and re-welcome them into community. Sometimes, I doubt we can really understand what these people would have experienced…or perhaps, maybe we can. Let me read to you from a book by Max Lucado. In it, he has a reflection on the leper in today's Gospel story.

For five years no one touched me. No one. Not one person. Not my wife. Not my child. Not my friends. No one touched me. They saw me. They spoke to me. I sensed love in their voices. I saw concern in their eyes. But I didn't feel their touch. There was no touch. Not once. No one touched me.

What is common to you, I coveted. Handshakes. Warm embraces. A tap on the shoulder to get my attention. A kiss on the lips to steal a heart. Such moments were taken from my world. No one touched me. No one bumped into me. What I would have given to be bumped into, to be caught in a crowd, for my shoulder to brush against another's. But for five years, it has not happened. How could it? I was not allowed on the streets. Even the rabbis kept their distance from me. I was not permitted in my synagogue. Not even welcomed in my own house.

I was untouchable. I was a leper. And no one touched me...until today.[10]

I wonder as Jesus healed so many of these people, how it affected HIM. So often we think about the one healed...but I wonder:

When crutches were thrown away, did Jesus limp? Did His eyes dim when the blind could see? Did his life weaken, when Jairus' daughter was awakened? Did scales appear on His skin, as the leper was healed? The Gospels said "Power went out of him" but as power went out, did pain come in?[11]

And even if all of these were true, did He ever cease to heal, even after His death?

Imagine what it would be like if We had that healing power of Jesus. If we, like the psalmist in Psalm 32 were able to pardon the sins of the diseased, and grant them healing. I wonder....who are the lepers in our lives? Who are the ones who are untouchable? And what if we COULD heal them? Would we? What if it meant our pride would limp, our image of what we think we are might dim; some pain might enter in, and even perhaps for a moment we might live in the shoes of that leper.

What if We could heal a Leper? Would we? Because if we wanted to...if we *want* to, WE CAN.

---

10 Max Lucado, *Just Like Jesus. (Nashville TN: Word Publishing, 1998). 28-29.*

11 John Shea, *Eating with the Bridegroom: The Spiritual Wisdom of the Gospels for Christian Preachers and Teachers. (Collegeville, MN: Liturgical Press, 2004). 58-59.*

Seventh Sunday in Tempus per Annum (Cycle B)
(Isaiah 43:18-19, 21-22, 24b-25; 2 Corinthians 1:18-22; Mark 2:1-12)

"Lord, heal my soul"

Sometimes, it is easier to say, "Rise, pick up your mat, and go home." The "sins are forgiven" thing is a tough one. One of the most common complaints among non-Catholic Christians and Catholics as well is "Why must I go to confession? Why can't I confess my sins directly to God." The answer to this question is quite easy. Sure you could confess your sins directly to God… but why would you want to?

Jesus knew the burden of sin. Jesus also knew that people needed a fleshy face on God at times in their life, most especially those times when they could not possibly believe that they could be forgiven. They would need not only a fleshy face, but one with authority; one with mercy; one who would let them know forgiveness.

Isaiah says it beautifully: "Remember not the events of the past, the things of long ago consider not; see, I am doing something new!" That's what it's about. We have a God of Second chance. And yet we can't seem to believe it. We might begin to understand if we knew that "God delights in forgiving. Forgiveness is the completion of love."[12] Benedict XVI states in *Deus Caritas Est*: "God's passionate love for his people – for humanity – is at the same time a forgiving love. It is so great that it turns God against Himself, his love against his justice."[13] "Lord, heal my soul, for I have sinned against you." But there are some things which are God will not do. God will not forgive us, if we do not want forgiveness. And sometimes, it is that which keeps us in our paralysis…keeps us from being healed.

---

12 Fr. Peter van Breeman. *The God Who Won't Let Go.* (Notre Dame, IN: Ave Maria Press, 1991), 60.

13 *Pope Benedict XVI. Deus Caritas Est. Encyclical Letter. (Vatican City: Libreria Editrice Vaticana, 2006). §10.*

FIRST SUNDAY OF LENT
(CYCLE B)
(GENESIS 9:8-15; 1 PETER 3:18-22; MARK 1: 12-15)

Are we keeping the Covenant?

"See, I set my bow in the clouds to serve as a sign of the covenant between me and the earth." The bow He placed in the sky as a sign is translated from the Hebrew word *keshet*, which is a war bow. God is placing his war bow in the sky...essentially hanging up His weapon as a sign that it will not be used. A covenant we wish for Him to keep. But with every covenant comes a responsibility, not only on the giver, but the receiver as well.

Every sacrament is a gift, but a gift with responsibility because it is also a covenant. Which one of you would ever entrust your child to someone, if you didn't believe they would take care of them *as you* would...or at least try? Which of you would lend money to someone who told you they were simply going to waste it? They were not going to invest it into something worthwhile, but simply squander it. Which of you would take the time to teach someone a trade or a craft if you knew they had no intention of following through with it or at the very least using it for the good of another?

Such is the case with our God. A God who has made us with certain gifts and abilities far exceeding anything we could have ever hoped for or imagined. He entrusts us with, not only our own gifts, but the gifts of others as well, with the sure hope that we will invest those gifts towards His purpose, but with no assurance that such will be the case...and yet He trusts.

Imagine what it must have been like for Christ. Given all this power and immediate stardom and yet the first thing he does is go out to be alone. What's interesting is that Mark puts it in the purest terms: "The Spirit drove (threw out) Jesus out into the desert." The Greek actually reads *ekballo*, which means was "thrown out" into the desert. Strong language for the Son of Man. Yet it leads us to believe he wasn't walking there on his own. He had to be driven to the desert, because it was there that he would begin to fulfil the will of the Father, and further the covenant we would have through him. It was after his Baptism (a sacrament for us) that he does this. With any gift comes responsibility, and so what are we to do?

Look at our relationship with God and ask the question…how well are we holding up our end of the bargain. In the next few weeks of Lent, as we approach the celebration of the *Triduum* we will discuss how we can become new creatures, if we have been the creatures we'd always hoped we would not become.

Second Sunday of Lent
(Cycle B)
Genesis 22:1-2, 9a, 10-13, 15-18; Romans 8: 31b-34; Mark 9:2-10)

"You are a child of the Light. May you keep the flame of faith alive…"

Every sacrament is a gift, but a gift with responsibility because it is also a covenant. We are baptized, but are we really a member of the Church or someone who visits on occasion? In the baptismal prayer over the parents we hear: "You are the first teachers of your children in the ways of the faith…may you also be the best of teachers." The responsibility of Baptism is on the one baptized and those who are responsible for that life. The covenant does not end with the ritual, but is eternal.

Once we enter into covenant with God, that *IS* our relationship with him. Abraham is a perfect example of this from the first reading. Abraham entered into a covenant with God, not really realizing all that the covenant would demand, and yet, he entered into it faithfully, with full hope that God would never ask anything but the best. You can imagine the shock, when God requested the one thing Abraham valued most. Having waited so long for a son of his own flesh, and having now to surrender that son. However, it was with a trusting faith that he offered even his son, and God rewarded him for his faithfulness.

Baptism is a reenactment of that covenant. We offer our child to the Lord with the hope that the Lord will bless that child. But we don't simply offer the child for that day…we offer them for eternity. And God will bless that child, but it is up to us to uphold our responsibility and keep the child close to God. Paul says it best: "If God is for us, who can be against us?" It's true. If we offer everything we have to the Father, we really, need nothing.

Jesus' own baptism is echoed on the mountain in the transfiguration. God validates all his son has done through his words, and yet the validation does not end with a glorious victory over an evil empire; it does not result in Christ's exaltation. The conclusion of this transfiguration is Jesus turning his face towards Jerusalem and speaking about his impending death. The sacrament leads to sacrifice. Without the sacrifice; without the efforts to fulfil our responsibility, we cannot grow closer to God, and in fact are driven away from Him through sin. But even then... even when we shirk our responsibility; even when we separate ourselves from Him, he still, is faithful to us. For he gave us another sacrament, that like baptism, forgives sins and brings us back into communion with Him. That sacrament is reconciliation. So next week we will explore how this sacrament allows us to empty ourselves so that we might fully receive our Lord.

THIRD SUNDAY OF LENT
(CYCLE B)
(EXODUS 20:1-17; 1 CORINTHIANS 1:22-25; JOHN 2:13-25)

Has the house been cleaned in preparation for the entry of our Lord?

"The foolishness of God is wiser than human wisdom, and the weakness of God is stronger than human strength." But how can we know what it is that God wants of us? How is it we are to discern our purpose? We follow a map. I don't know about you, but for me reading directions, or asking for directions sometimes feels like defeat. Perhaps that's pride on my part (not really, but probably). I would much rather take five hours to put something together than to stop and read through the directions. In the same vein, I would rather drive for miles and try to do it myself, than to stop and ask directions, or listen to an *over-zealous back-seat driver*. Pride again? Perhaps. At any rate, there seems to be something within our human nature that inhibits such logic as asking for help or depending on something outside of ourselves. That is what gets us into trouble.

God gives us the map...gives us the directions to find that peace and fulfillment. These laws or commands are given to us in the book of Exodus. Interesting, isn't it, that the book of Exodus is about the escape route from slavery. Isn't it ironic that those commandments that come from Exodus give us, not only a simple road map for our life and discovering our purpose, but also give us the escape route from slavery. So why don't we take it? For the same reason that the Pharisees didn't listen to Jesus.

"What sign can you show us for doing this?" What did he do? He "cleaned house" essentially. I suppose it was His house to clean, but nonetheless, he cleaned out all the stuff that had crept in over the centuries. We've done it too at times. We've forgotten that the sanctuary in our church IS the *Holy of Holies*. We let anyone traipse through, put up trees around it and all sorts of stuff. The house can

46

get cluttered after awhile. "Where are you going with this?" You're wondering right?

In the ancient world, our heart was the domus (translated from Latin, house). This is the house, our heart. That's where we get the word *ab-domen*, away from the house. So how about that. Our house gets cluttered over time. Why does this happen? For the same reason it takes fifteen hours to put together that bike that said "some assembly required." For the same reason it takes us ten hours to get to Pittsburgh instead of the four that is suggested. We haven't read the directions... we don't have the map. It's not as if we don't have access to these things, but we just choose not to.

We have the map...we were given the directions...they are written in our hearts (the *domus*) but perhaps it's been sometime since we've looked at them. So what can we do. We can allow Jesus to do now, what he did back then. Let him "clean house." Let him cleanse our house of all that has crept in over time. This is so important, that he made it a sacrament. This reconciliation is not only a house cleaning, but more importantly, it pulls us back on the right path.

Think of it like this. Our relationship with God is like a rope. When we turn away, we sever that rope, that connection and move away from the one force which anchors us, which is God. The longer the separation exists the further we move away from God. But when we turn back; when we try to reconcile, then God reaches out; grabs our end of the rope and ties a knot. And you know, that a rope once cut, and then retied is shorter than it once was. And therefore, each time we turn back to God and He ties the knot, He also draws us in closer and closer to Him.

He made it a sacrament because he knew we would need more than a simple confession to the wind, or in the privacy of our home. He knew we would need the human face of God. We invite Him in and he will clean the house. And once clean, that is the perfect disposition to welcome him in, as we do when we receive him in the Eucharist.

We have received the sacrament of reconciliation but when was the last time? Are we allowing ourselves to be forgiven; are we offering that one sin that we hold so sacred and are unwilling to unload? Perhaps we have received the Eucharist, or have been receiving the Eucharist. But are we properly disposed to receive Jesus into our house? Has our temple been cleansed in preparation for our Lord? For each week he echoes the words he once spoke to Zacchaeus: "I wish to stay at your house today" (*Luke 19:5*). So that he might also echo the words: "Today, salvation has come to this house."

FOURTH SUNDAY OF LENT
(CYCLE B)
(2 CHRONICLES 36:14-16, 19-23; EPHESIANS 2: 4-10; JOHN 3:14-21)

Do we avoid the light or simply linger in the darkness.

We have a natural attraction to light. In the science world, we would be called *phototropic* (light feeding). Even plants react to this, as they grow toward the light. But as phototropic as we might be, sometimes we reject that which gives life.

In the *Dialogues* of Plato, he gives an allegory or word picture for the human condition. He speaks of creatures in a cave. These creatures are chained by the neck and leg so they can neither move, nor look about. They are given the basic needs of nourishment and water, but no touch. They are simply kept alive in absolute darkness. But there is a fire in the background and every now and then they can see shadows of figures passing in front of the fire. That is all they see.

Then he poses the question: what if one of the prisoners were set free? All they have known is the protection and darkness of the cave, and these obscure shadows. So at first they would have to be forced to stand. This would be quite painful, if not torturous that after years of living in that position they would have to use muscles they never had to use before. Once standing, they might also have to be lead toward the mouth of the cave, not wanting to go there themselves. As they approached the light, it would burn their eyes that had never seen light, and their skin would immediately feel the heat. Furthermore, as they exited the entrance to the cave, the light would feel as hot coals placed into their eyes and their skin would feel as though it were on fire. But....after awhile....after having adjusted to these new harsh conditions, there would be ecstasy.[14] To imagine seeing so many shapes, colors, so much movement and light. The creature might feel for the first time as though they are really living....they might be tempted to worship the one who brought them out of the darkness amidst the pain

49

and suffering that was first present.   That is grace. But what of the others?

Paul says to the Ephesians: *For by grace you have been saved through faith, and this is not from you; it is the gift of God; it is not from works, so no one may boast.* Now, out of the cave, what is the obligation of this creature to the prisoners back there in the darkness? Certainly the one who freed him would not also ask that he return to the cave, right? Those who are given sight would never want to return to blindness, right? But those in the cave would never willingly come to the surface. What if he went back, and he was mocked roundly....what if they refused to come with him.....what if they came with him, but the pain was too great and killed them, or worse, drove them mad?

> *The light came into the world, but people preferred darkness to light, because their works were evil. For everyone who does wicked things hates the light and does not come toward the light, so that his works might not be exposed. But whoever lives the truth comes to the light, so that his works may be clearly seen as done in God.*

Why would anyone choose to remain in the cave? Why would anyone fear the light? I remember one time while in college, I decided to paint my bedroom at home. Growing up in my parents' house, I had used the room to its full potential...I mean **used** it. So I decided I would do the work. I filled in all the holes in the walls (and there were quite a few of those) and spackled and smoothed and sanded. Then when it was time to paint, I wanted to do the best I could, so I removed all the receptacles, face plates from the lights and the wall lights. I taped over the windows and was ready to begin. Since I had no lights, what with the windows taped and the ceiling lights gone, I put a desk lamp in the middle of the room and began my work. I did everything to the letter, and finally after a few days had finished the job. It looked magnificent! I was truly proud of the job I had done, and so I put all the face plates back on, along with the ceiling lights and was ready to move back all the furniture. I turned on the ceiling light and..... Horror! There were places where the paint had dripped down a wall, or a corner; there were places where I had missed a second coat and the color was different. There were places where I had filled holes and it looked like a stucco wall! It was ruined....why didn't I see these things when the desk lamp was turned on? So I had to make a decision. The decision was this: I could either paint the room again, making sure I took care of all my variables ...or....just use dim lights in here for the rest of my time.

See, to live in the light gives us beauty, depth, and shows us reality, but is often painful to the eyes at times, and a great deal of work. There are animals on this planet that have been in the dark so long, they no longer have eyes. Some of us can get like that too. We decide it's much easier to live in the dim light which covers all sorts of flaws and weakness. Worse yet, some choose to remain in the cave. They've heard what it's like outside of the cave, but are comfortable where they are. And so, in days ahead they will lose use of their eyes, and perhaps, even if brought out of the cave, will lose the ability to see...then it's too late. Then they have reached the absolute poverty.

This *Laetare* Sunday is a movement out of the cave. It is the glimmer of light that can be seen amidst all the darkness, and an invitation to look at our lives, and the lives around us, and to emerge from a darkness, or darknesses that we have been satisfied to wallow in....that have crept over us in the years past, and to emerge in the light, which for awhile causes pain, only to welcome us into the ecstasy of reality. And then to return, only to draw others into the light as well. You might be wondering: "What did he do? Re-paint the whole room again, or just use dim lights in there the rest of the time?" Ha! I'll never tell.

---

14 Plato, Republic: Book VII, page 186-188, transl. By G.M.A. Grube, (Cambridge: Hackett Publishing Company, Inc., 1992), 186-188.

FIFTH SUNDAY OF LENT
(CYCLE B)
(JEREMIAH 31:31-34; HEBREWS 5:7-9; JOHN 12:20-33)

The meaning of L-E-N-T

Love's Embrace Never Takes......it gives. Jesus says: *"He who loses his life will gain it, and he who clings to his life will lose it."* Jesus could never had said such words; his words would never have endured, had he not surrendered *his* life. Love's Embrace Never Takes. If we believe that love is the inherent ability to give our lives to another...to give ourselves as a gift to another, then this will always lead to a loss of life. Think about it... if love is self gift, then we put our focus on others. And if we do this, and do it to the highest level, then we begin to forget ourselves. Fulton Sheen has said, "this highest level of this 'self-forgetfulness' is a loss of life."[15] *"Is there any greater love than to lay down one's life for one's friends?"* What can be greater than to offer our life to someone?

What is greater is to offer this love....to offer our lives...even to those who don't want it. This is the law that is spoken of by Jeremiah. *"I will write my law in their hearts...not like my covenant long ago."* Long ago, it was enough to love and offer our lives for those we love.... but for our enemies? That is too much to take...right? But Love's Embrace Never Takes. So what must we do?

When class started, the professor pulled out a big box of donuts. No, these weren't the normal kinds of donuts, they were the extra fancy BIG kind, with cream centers and frosting swirls. Everyone was pretty excited. It was Friday, the last class of the day, and they were going to get an early start on the weekend with a party in Dr. Christianson's class. Dr. Christianson went to the first girl in the first row and asked, "Cynthia, do you want to have one of these donuts?" Cynthia said, "Yes." Dr. Christianson then turned to Steve and asked, "Steve, would you do ten push-ups so that Cynthia can have a donut? "Sure." Steve jumped down from his desk to do a quick ten. Then Steve again sat in his desk. Dr. Christianson put a donut on Cynthia's desk. Dr. Christianson then went to Joe, the next person, and asked, "Joe, do you want a donut?" Joe said, "Yes." Dr. Christianson asked, "Steve would you do ten push-ups so Joe can have a donut?" Steve did ten push-ups, Joe got a donut.

And so it went, down the first aisle, Steve did ten pushups for every person before they got their donut. Walking down the second aisle, Dr. Christianson came to Scott. Scott was on the basketball team, and in as good condition as Steve. He was very popular and never lacking for female companionship. When the professor asked, "Scott do you want a donut?" Scott's reply was, "Well, can I do my own pushups?" Dr. Christianson said, "No, Steve has to do them." Then Scott said, "Well, I don't want one then." Dr. Christianson shrugged and then turned to Steve and asked, "Steve, would you do ten pushups so Scott can have a donut he doesn't want?" With perfect obedience Steve started to do ten pushups. Scott said, "HEY! I said I didn't want one!" Dr. Christianson said, "Look!, this is my classroom, my class, my desks, and these are my donuts. Just leave it on the desk if you don't want it." And he put a donut on Scott's desk. Now by this time, Steve had begun to slow down a little. He just stayed on the floor between sets because it took too much effort to be getting up and down. You could start to see a little perspiration coming out around his brow. Dr. Christianson started down the third row. Now the students were beginning to get a little angry. Dr. Christianson asked Jenny, "Jenny, do you want a donut?" Sternly, Jenny said, "No." Then Dr. Christianson asked Steve, "Steve, would you do ten more push-ups so Jenny can have a donut that she doesn't want?" Steve did ten....Jenny got a donut. By now, a growing sense of uneasiness filled the room. The students were beginning to say "No" and there were all these uneaten donuts on the desks. Steve also had to really put forth a lot of extra effort to get these pushups done for each donut. There began to be a small pool of sweat on the floor beneath his face, his arms and brow were beginning to get red because of the physical effort involved. Dr. Christianson asked Robert, who was the most vocal unbeliever in the class, to watch Steve do each push up to make sure he did the full ten pushups in a set because he couldn't bear to watch all of Steve's work for all of those uneaten donuts. He sent Robert over to where Steve was so Robert could count the set and watch Steve closely. Dr. Christianson started down the fourth row. During his class, however, some students from other classes had wandered in and sat down on the steps along the radiators that ran down the sides of the room. When the professor realized this, he did a quick count and saw that now there were thirty-four students in the room. He started to worry if Steve would be able to make it.   Dr. Christianson went on to the next person and the next and the next.

Near the end of that row, Steve was really having a rough time. He was taking a lot more time to complete each set. Steve asked Dr Christianson, "Do I have to make my nose touch on each one?" Dr. Christianson thought for a moment, "Well, they're your pushups. You are in charge now. You can do them any way that you want." And Dr. Christianson went on. A few moments later, Jason, a recent transfer student, came to the room and was about to come in when all the students yelled in one voice, "NO! Don't come in! Stay out!" Jason didn't know what was going on. Steve picked up his head and said, "No, let him come." Professor Christianson said, "You realize that if Jason comes in you will have to do ten pushups for him?" Steve said, "Yes, let him come in. Give him a donut" Dr. Christianson said, "Okay, Steve, I'll let you get Jason's out of the way right now. Jason, do you want a donut?" Jason, new to the room, hardly knew what was going on. "Yes," he said, "give me a donut." "Steve, will you do ten push-ups so that Jason can have a donut?" Steve did ten pushups very slowly and with great effort. Jason, bewildered, was handed a donut and sat down. Dr. Christianson finished the fourth row, and then started on those visitors seated by the heaters. Steve's arms were now shaking with each push-up in a struggle to lift himself against the force of gravity. By this time sweat was profusely dropping off of his face, there was no sound except his heavy breathing; there was not a dry eye in the room. The very last two students in the room were two young women, both cheerleaders, and very popular. Dr. Christianson went to Linda, the second to last, and asked, "Linda, do you want a doughnut?" Linda said, very sadly, "No, thank you." Professor Christianson quietly asked, "Steve, would you do ten push-ups so that Linda can have a donut she doesn't want?" Grunting from the effort, Steve did ten very slow pushups for Linda. Then Dr Christianson turned to the last girl, Susan. "Susan, do you want a donut?" Susan, with tears flowing down her face, began to cry. "Dr. Christianson, why can't I help him?" Dr. Christianson said, "No, Steve has to do it alone, I have given him this task and he is in charge of seeing that everyone has an opportunity for a donut whether they want it or not.

When I decided to have a party this last day of class, I looked at my grade book. Steve here is the only student with a perfect grade. Everyone else has failed a test, skipped class, or offered me inferior work. Steve told me that in football practice, when a player messes up he must do push-ups. I told Steve that none of you could come to my party unless he paid the price by doing your push ups. He and I made a deal for your sakes." "Steve, would you do ten push-ups so Susan can have a donut?" As Steve very slowly finished his last pushup, with the understanding that he had accomplished all that was required of him, having done 350 pushups, his arms buckled beneath him and he fell to the floor. Dr. Christianson turned to the room and said. "And so it was, that our Savior, Jesus Christ, on the cross, pleaded to the Father, 'into thy hands I commend my spirit.' With the understanding that He had done everything that was required of Him, He yielded up His life. And like some of those in this room, many of us leave the gift on the desk, uneaten."[16]

This *is* love's embrace. That Jesus offered his suffering, his very life…and He received nothing! That some wanted the salvation offered, while others did not…and yet he suffered for all, so that perhaps those who had not wanted the salvation initially, might have changed their mind and be able to receive it.

This is a difficult saying though….how can anyone love like that? How can anyone experience a Love's Embrace that Never Takes? They must learn it, because it has been forgotten or glossed over. But it is still written on our hearts. We must go through a period when we ask forgiveness of our wrongs, and learn to forgive those who have wronged us. We must meditate on this wonderful sacrifice our God has offered for us, and then having gone through this process, we experience life in a new way, and can learn to love even those who have wronged *us*. What is this process…the words make up the process through which we must pass to experience them. Love's Embrace Never Takes. L-E-N-T. We call this process…this journey…. Lent.

15 Bishop Fulton J. Sheen, The World's First Love, (New York, NY: McGraw-Hill Co., 1952), 120.
16 Forwarded Story from the Internet

PALM SUNDAY (CYCLE B)
(ISAIAH 50:4-7; PHILIPPIANS 2: 6-11; MARK 14:1-15:47)

What say you to our Lord?

Jesus is in the garden and asks the apostles to stay with him for an hour and pray. Now I don't know about you, but I was one of those people who didn't "get" the whole sleepover thing when I was younger. We'd get our sleeping bags all set up; we'd get situated with a movie, or chat or whatever. And for whatever reason, it took only a matter of minutes before I would fall asleep. I was the worst "slumber party person" in the world…perhaps you can relate.

The only time this habit of falling into listless sleep right away was suspended, was if one of my friends really needed to talk. I would have to try with all my might, but I did it. I imagine you would do it as well. Think back to that moment. The last moment in the garden of Gethsemane. Jesus asks YOU to stay awake with him for one hour. This is our Lord. This is the one who has given us all; and then on top of that eternal life. What would you say to him if he asked you this moment? Because every week he asks your company. Not sleeping in the garden, but present active participation in his prayer. He asks an hour from you, his closest friend. What will you say now?

EASTER VIGIL
(CYCLE ABC)
(GENESIS 1:1-2:2; EXODUS 14:15-15:1; ISAIAH 55:1-11; ROMANS 6:3-11; MARK 16:1-7)

"He is risen as He said."

Today we celebrate the highest point in the Church year. But I would be remiss if I didn't recount what has occurred in the days preceding this one. It would be like reading the final chapter, without knowing what the rest of the book was about.

On Holy Thursday we commemorated our reception of the greatest gift the Lord has given us....Himself. He gave the Eucharist to all of his disciples and then washed their feet, even knowing that one would betray him, one would deny him and the rest would desert him. From there we followed him into the garden which would begin his passion on Good Friday. Having been deserted by those he loved, he begins his journey in solitude. *Smitten and scourged for our offenses.* And yet as he takes his last breath, breathing forgiveness he gasps: *"It is finished."* He rejected all temptation and overcame the evil one, perfectly and completely, dying between two thieves. This should not surprise us, because "the Church is always God hung between two thieves."[17] But this is not the end. And so we celebrate that after three days in the tomb, after his repose in the tomb on the seventh day, the Sabbath; the eighth day, He IS RISEN!

And so tonight we celebrate much as they did 1970 years ago. We gather in the catacombs and crypts; gather in caves and barns; gather in houses and yards to celebrate the victory of the *Light* over the darkness, and to bring into the Body of Christ its newest members. This is the Eighth day...the first day of true living life!

Those catechumens who were to be baptized arrived in their birthday suits! (But for the sake of decency tonight, we've allowed them to dress.) They were brought in front of the congregation, having passed the scrutinies and been instructed in the faith. They were then taken to a pool which had eight sides. Listen to the Gospel: *"On the first day of the week, after the Sabbath."* From this day forward, it will no longer be the first day, but the eighth day! In the creation story we heard, God made everything in six days, on the seventh day He rested, and then on the eighth day, was the first day that we lived in creation. So tonight as these catechumens are baptized, as they die with Christ they rise a new creation.....it is the eighth day! For this reason, many of the older baptismal fonts are eight sided. The eighth day, is the day we received the gift of life.

After emerging as new creatures, having been forgiven any sins of their past life and the original sin from the beginning, they now begin their new life. But along with those who were previously baptized they will receive the gifts of the Holy Spirit, as Jesus was anointed before going into the desert to combat the evil one, so now you will be given the graces. In Genesis we heard *"God breathed over the waters."* The word they translate as "breath" is *Ruach*. The same word that is used for the Holy Spirit. And God said "Let us make man in our *Image* and *Likeness"*, so our journey continues with the Breath of God. As you receive the Holy Spirit you will feel the joy of discovering "that you bear the fingerprints of God on your bodies and His breath in your soul."[18] You will be anointed with Chrism, the oil used to anoint priests, prophets, and kings. Just as Jesus the *Messiah*, the *Christos*, the *Anointed*, so you are called to be Christ to each other. Christ who never judged or condemned anyone, except those who thought they needed him not.

And so having been empowered with these gifts and the Spirit in your soul, you will be activists for the faith. For as God said to Moses, *"Why are you crying out to me?! Get up and MOVE!!"* That you will not be lukewarm in your faith but convicted; that the *kerygma* which *is* our faith will move you to change the world, with nothing less than your example. For Jesus who baptizes *"with the Holy Spirit and Fire"* will ignite in your hearts a fire, not unlike the pillar that led the Israelites. With this fire you will lead others to seek and find; to knock and open; to ask and receive. Therefore, those who were baptized were given a candle from the Easter fire. Although the whole church was illumined by the candles of many, all lit from that one flame, the original flame was never diminished. Such is the case with our faith. As long as your spread the Word wherever you go, it will be as a font inside of you. Then as the vigil continued all night (as it will not tonight) sunrise could come. And these homes and churches, even cemeteries oriented facing the east would catch the first glimmers of *son-light* through the open doors, so that at the consecration, the sun would hit the altar. THIS IS OUR FAITH! KERYGMA!

This...is the night. Oh happy fault of Adam. But remember this night, because there will be times, once down from the mountain, when we might be tempted to forget. When the pressures of life can begin to breathe fear into our hearts. But *do not let your hearts be troubled.* Mary approaches the tomb with the other Mary on the eighth day. As the angel approaches the guards are as dead men. Isn't it ironic that those who were living, appeared as dead, and the one who was to be dead WAS NOW ALIVE! And as Mary approaches she will experience *de-javous.* For the phrase the angel voiced to a young virgin at the beginning of her journey into motherhood, he would now repeat at the end of her journey as a childless widow, *"Do not be afraid."* They were *seeking the dead among the living.* We cannot afford to make that same mistake. If we do, then we are worse off than those who do not believe at all. *WE* become the atheists who attend Church, and the Gospel becomes no more than myths and stories that children may read. We need something to hold onto. Something that in the midst of solitude and isolation we feel connected, we feel alive. That even through the darkness our hand is grasped by another. That is *Kerygma.*

When I was about eight or nine years old (they all blend together when you get older) I decided "That's it! I've had it! I'm going to run away." I packed my suitcase with all the essentials: candy, toys, and one change of clothes; grabbed my stuffed leopard and put him on my shoulders and was ready to head out into the snow. And as I approached the door to make my exit into the wilderness, there she was.....my mother. She said: "What are you doing?" I replied, "I'm running away." I had anticipated such an encounter yet my response that I was running away just didn't have the vigor it had when I rehearsed it. But the next thing she said absolutely floored me. "Where are your boots?" she asked. My boots? What was this all about? I said, "I can't find them." And then she said, "You can't run away until you find your boots." "What?!!" What just happened here? I was running away. And this was just the reason I was doing it. You can't enforce laws and pull rank when someone's running away. You can't do that. I was speechless for a moment, and then repeated my assertion: "I'm running away." And just as solid as ever she retorted, "Well you can just put down that suitcase and leopard, because you're not going anywhere until you find your boots, and that's final." It wasn't fair! I wanted so badly to run away, and yet I couldn't do it because I couldn't find my dumb boots! I looked all morning and almost got to the point where I had forgotten why I was even looking for them, when I smelled something wonderful cooking. And when I came into the kitchen a nice lunch was waiting for me and my siblings. And I realized perhaps I didn't have it too bad. Although I have my suspicions, I never found out whether or not my mother actually hid my boots, but I do know mothers have been known to do such things.

The fact is, I might have run away (although I wouldn't have gotten very far) if it weren't for someone who loved me enough to keep me there, even with something as insignificant as boots. I speak to those who have just been brought into the Church recently; to those who have remained here for years, having not run away even when tempted to; to those who have come back after years of being away; to those who are passing through. "Welcome Home." We are all a part of each other whether we like it or not....so we might as well like it. And so we have an obligation to go out of our way, to support those who in isolation or solitude or through pain, might feel inclined to go away from the Church; to run away from the family. And tonight and all through the year we are given these signs and symbols; we are given nights like this one where we feel so at one with one another and so much a part of something greater than ourselves that we can hold on through those tough times.

YOU be the mothers for these who have none; you be the mothers who keep the children of God in the home, even when tempted to run away. Be not afraid. *"Jesus is risen as he said."* And if this is true, then everything else he said and did is also fulfilled. *"Do not let your hearts be troubled. The Father wishes that I should not lose any of whom He gave me. But that I will raise them up on the last day."* Now, with that *Kerygma* which is our faith, Go and be that change YOU seek in the World.

---

17 *Fr. Ronald Rolheiser, OMI, The Holy Longing: The Search for a Christian Spirituality, (New York: Doubleday, 1999), 128.*

18 *Fr. Warren Murrman OSB, Homily given in St. Gregory Chapel, at St. Vincent Seminary, Latrobe PA, 2001.*

SECOND SUNDAY OF EASTER
(CYCLE B)
(ACTS 4:32-35; 1 JOHN 5:1-6; JOHN 20: 19-31)

From L-I-P to T-A-I-L.

"In this way we know that we love the children of God, when we love God and obey his commandments." In this, we find purpose and in this we find peace. So people will often say: "Father, when you preach, make it practical. Make it something I can use in my daily life." I believe this is what everyone is looking for. If you question this look at the self-help section of any bookstore. Look at the salaries of the motivational speakers, etc. Now when I was younger, I read *Dianetics*, by L. Ron Hubbard. And now I'm glad I did, so I can dissuade others from wasting their time. I read, *How to Make Friends and Influence People,* by Dale Carnegie. I read *The Seven Habits of Highly Effective People*. And you know what? It was meaningless. All those things I read in those books, I now know, and employ, but it wasn't because of anything I read in those books. It was two other books that I read, which helped me. The first book was the Bible....the second....the Catechism of the Catholic Church.

Now, before you turn me off, just give me another second or two for the *pitch*. If you're gonna listen to Tony Little, or Dale Carnegie, at least give me a shake. Having spoken to hundreds of people (many of you), I have compiled my own list: "The seven habits of Holy Happy people." These aren't necessarily things people had listed to me, but when I asked them, what's going well in life, these are the things that were mentioned most often.

1. See life through the **Lens** of God. When you wake up, your first action should be thanksgiving...morning offering. The Psalmist shouts: *Give thanks to the Lord for He is good, His love is everlasting.* Quick, and painless, it devotes your whole day to God. The Sign of the Cross is important for this. Think about it. Whenever we make the sign of the cross "In the name of the Father and of the

Son and of the Holy Spirit," then anything we do that follows, is done in their name. And therefore it's only the best we can do. Whenever making a decision ask yourself, is this what God wants? Our lives would change.

2. Intercession: Pray for people. So often our prayer is empty because it's just for us, so we can do it half-heartedly. Pray for people as though their lives depended on it. But if we had someone praying for *us*, how would we want them to pray? While driving their car or walking the dog? Should they pray for our intention while exercising or mowing the grass? Or should they come to the church; should they be in the presence of God? Would it be enough for them to pray standing or on their knees or on their belly? That is what intercessory prayer does. If we want people to pray for us in that way, then WE should pray for others. As if their lives depend on it.

3. Pray as a family at morning and night: Some would say this is impossible with our schedule. Perhaps there's too much in the schedule. In some religious traditions the day stops at morning and night, and everyone together offers prayers. The apostles were gathered together in the upper room when Jesus came. If every family prayed together, how powerful would that be?

4. Tithe: This is a tough one, and the thing I want to talk about least is money. But in my experience, and those of others, when I do not tithe (10%) I never have enough money. I'm always worried about security or where it will come from. Acts of the Apostles, "No one claimed that any of his possessions was his own, but they had everything in common" (*Acts 4:32*). When I do tithe, and when I do give freely, I always have more than enough. It's true.

5. Attend Mass every Sunday and Holy Day of obligation....at least. Jesus appeared to the apostles in the upper room together. He did not appear to Thomas alone. He appeared to two on the road to Emmaus. We must celebrate together. This is non-negotiable.

The worst thing we ever taught our kids is that going to Mass is a good thing, a holy thing, but not non-negotiable. Some believe "If it's inconvenient, it's okay to miss Mass." Imagine if our Lord had that attitude when it came to our issues. This does not mean going to Mass, and then talking on your cell during the homily, or going out for a cigarette. This doesn't mean always arriving after the beginning or leaving before the last hymn/prayer. It means a commitment.

6. Become **Involved** in the community. Many complain that the parish is cold, that they know no one, that they don't feel involved...well, Dale Carnegie would say, get involved. THIS IS NOT PART OF THE TITHE. Don't say I give my time as a tithe. There are no volunteers in the Church, we are all of one mind and heart, and so we work toward the common good...that is a responsibility. Even if it means going to coffee and donuts. There was a study done that said, going to these things can increase your income by 10% (there's the tithe). How? Networking.

7. **Laugh**! We can be some of the most solemn people in the world. There is this picture called "The laughing Jesus" and I heard this man say one time, that the picture was obscene. What? Did Jesus never laugh? I get an angry letter from someone....yep I get them, I know that's hard to believe.....SEE? Laughter, it's fantastic.

These things that I say....you might ask, where is the validity? If you can't find what I say in the two books I mentioned then discard them. I issue this challenge. Try this for ninety days (three months). You must do all Seven Habits for ninety days. If you do this, you will have peace and your life will be holier. If I'm wrong, then you can stop and you've lost nothing. If I'm right...then you might for the first time understand the resurrection. You will feel what Thomas did when he probed the wounds of the divine. And then you need not trod past the self-help section ever again.

Third Sunday of Easter
(Cycle B)
(Acts 3: 13-15, 17-19; 1 John 2:1-5a; Luke 24:35-48)

Seeking out the Lost Part I

For part of our celebrations in the Season of Easter, I would like to focus on what it means to "seek the lost"; what it means that we are members of the Church of a *Good* Shepherd. I would venture to say that there is not one of us here today, who has not had someone in his or her family who has left the Catholic Church. Or, someone who has not formally left, but does not attend. Or, someone who is not Catholic, and yet it seems they're right there, but something is hindering them from making that step.

Peter says to us in Acts: *I know, brothers, you acted out of ignorance; just as your leaders did; but God has brought it to fulfillment.* So we must bring back the lost. Because if we have the truth; if we have the fullness of the faith, why would we not want to bring everyone into the Church? Why would we not want to share our faith with everyone? So why would anyone leave, or not attend, or be trepidacious?

Top Ten Reasons[19]

Catholics
1. Some disagree with Catholic Doctrine (Catholic and Non-Catholic)
What often happens is people disagree with their *understanding* of the Catholic doctrine. Many times, if that doctrine can be explained, they really find out that they had no problem with it in the first place.

2. Some are angry with the Church's standpoint on moral issues (Catholic and Non-Catholic)
Which moral issues? The ones we don't want to keep. We only seek

the changes in laws that we do not want to keep. But if they are seeking the truth, then we must present it in a firm and consistent way. "We have done more damage in the name of pastoral care than all the heresies of the early church."[20]

3. Some have been scandalized by the church's bad example (Catholic and Non-Catholic)
Fr. Landry says:
If the scandal caused by Judas was all that the members of the early Church focused on, the Church would have been finished before it even started to grow. Instead, the Church recognized that you don't judge something by *those who don't live it*, but by those who do. Instead of focusing on the one who betrayed, they focused on the other Eleven, on account of whose work, preaching, miracles, love for Christ, we are here today."[21]

This scandal is a huge hanger on which some will try to hang their justification for not practicing the faith. That's why holiness is so important. They need to find in all of us a reason for faith, a reason for hope, a reason for responding with love to the love of the Lord.

4. Some are apathetic
He stated, "Those who commit these types of scandals are guilty of the spiritual equivalent of murder," destroying other people's faith in God by their terrible example. But then he warned his listeners, "But I'm here among you to prevent something far worse for you. While those who give scandal are guilty of the spiritual equivalent of murder, those who take scandal -- who allow scandals to destroy their faith -- are guilty of spiritual suicide." [22]

5. Some are angry because they feel the church has abandoned them
I believe this was Luther's perception, and in many counts, he was right. What was the promise of Christ.... *"I will be with you always..."* (*Mt. 28:20*). there is no separating Christ and His Church.

6. Some are angry with God
Because they cannot understand His ways.

Non-Catholics not coming over?

1. Misconceptions about the Catholic Church
Some of these are propagated by Catholics who are ignorant

2. Prejudices against the Catholic Church
Much of this is media initiated, but also preached in some churches.

3. Family
Some won't enter the church for fear of their family's rejection, while others, because they've been incessantly pestered and nagged will never enter the Church; if for no other reason than spite.
Issues surrounding the "people within the church" not the Church. Much of this also stems from misunderstanding.

4. *Not being fed* syndrome (Catholic and Non-Catholic)
Not being fed spiritually, emotionally, socially, etc. We live in a society where we are constantly trying to satiate our appetite for stimuli. If you doubt this, ask if you don't change channels during commercials (unless they're entertaining). Mass is not entertainment....it's worship. If it's about you, you don't have to come to church for that. For this hour, it's about God. Imagine being fed while you're hiding in a crypt celebrating the Lord's supper in the first century.

So what can we do? After seeing Jesus; touching him; and feeding him, the disciples were still incredulous. They still had trouble believing. And yet he says to these who have difficulty believing: *"You are the witnesses, and are to preach these things in my name to all the nations, beginning in Jerusalem."* So we must be the witnesses, even though we struggle with our own faith. Paul says: *"Whoever keeps his word, the love of God is truly perfected in him.*" The Word is only any good, however, if it is spoken.

Having now identified the symptoms of why sheep leave the flock, or are reluctant to come in, next week we will talk about ways of engaging with these children so to allow them to discover the Word among them.

---

19 Based on readings from Patrick Madrid, Search and Rescue: How to bring your Family and Friends into-
   or Back into – The Catholic Church, (Manchester, NH: Sophia Institute Press, 2001), 53-78.

20 Quoted from Patrick Madrid in a talk given to the Priests of the Diocese of Harrisburg at the Continuing
   Education Workshop, Hunt Valley MD. 2006.

21 Fr. Roger J. Landry, A homily delivered at Espirito Santo parish, Fall River MA, Reprinted by the Catholic
   Educator's Resource Center, February 3, 2002.

22 St. Francis De Sales, as quoted Ibid.

FOURTH SUNDAY OF EASTER
(CYCLE B)
(ACTS 4:8-12; 1 JOHN 3: 1-2; JOHN 10: 11-18)

Seeking out the Lost Part II

Last Sunday, we had the Gospel in which Christ tells us to go out to all the nations....not just His own. That we have an obligation to reach out to the lost, those who have fallen away. That the largest organized religion in the United States is Roman Catholicism with sixty-five million members. The second largest religion is made up of forty million members. These are INACTIVE CATHOLICS. So we must reach out to these individuals to welcome them home.

We talked about the top ten reasons why people leave the Church, while on the other end of the spectrum there are non-Catholics are reluctant to enter the Church. I would like to talk today about two reasons Catholics leave the faith and non-Catholics are reluctant to enter the Church: Doctrinal issues and Major Misunderstandings of the Faith.

Catholics
7. Some disagree with Catholic Doctrine (Catholic and Non-Catholic) or misunderstand it. What often happens is people disagree <u>because of</u> their understanding of the Catholic doctrine. Many times, if that doctrine can be explained, they really had no problem with it in the first place. There are a few doctrines which will cause many Catholics to leave, and will prevent countless others who are not Catholic from joining the faith. The first is the statement made in Acts today by Peter: *"There is no salvation through anyone else, nor is there any other name under heaven given to the human race by which we are to be saved."*

This statement has been misconstrued in so many ways over the years that people will claim: "I refuse to be a part of a religion that discriminates against non-Christians." We have to understand this scripture in light of the tradition. (see document *Dominus Iesus*) There *IS* only salvation through Jesus Christ. What this means is that when we die, Jew or Greek, slave or free, etc. we will face our Judge (Jesus Christ) and it is only *through him* that we receive salvation.

Part of the concern, however, probably stems from a question of what occurs. Have you ever wondered why we pray for the dead? Think about it. If they're in heaven, they have no need of our prayers…if they're in hell, our prayers cannot help them. So why pray for them? Unless, there is something else…a purification. Although we are forgiven our sins through the sacrament of Reconciliation, there are scars that remain. We know that nothing that is impure can come within the sight of God and live. Therefore we need a purification.

Imagine that God is the flame…pure light. If I have a silver bar coated in wax and dirt and filth, as the bar moves closer to the flame what happens to the filth? It is burned away until the bar is next to the fire, but not consumed by it…and in its purest form. The form in which we were created from the beginning. Purgatory is not a negative thing. It is a journey toward the Divine. But here's the clincher. We must pray for those in Purgatory, because once in purgatory, or even heaven, one's will is so completely oriented toward God and *other*, that they cannot focus on *self*. Therefore, they can pray for US but they cannot pray for themselves. Most who disagree with this doctrine will complain that it is not in scripture. That leads into the third misunderstanding.

This last issue deals to the third greatest discrepancy, which is Tradition and Magisterium. If we only looked at the scripture in this case, we would have to eliminate most of the people from the earth as having the possibility of being saved. That is why we need tradition. Anyone can interpret scripture. We must realize the scriptures as we know them were not compiled in that order until almost 400 years after Christ. Who compiled it? The apostles' apostles' apostles' apostles....in other words, the *Magisterium* or teaching body of the Church. Without tradition and the Magisterium, the bible is liable to become a lie. Think about this sentence: **I didn't say you stole money.**[23] I can say this stressing different words a number of different ways. In the ancient languages it is pretty clear what it means. I can offer a good example as one of the greatest wedges into the solid foundation of the Church, even in the time of Jesus. The Eucharist.

John 6:51-60. Most non-Catholic Christians do not know this passage, or do not wish to know it. Let me read part of this to you.

ἀμὴν ἀμὴν λέγω ὑμῖν, ἐὰν μὴ **φάγητε** τὴν **σάρκα** τοῦ υἱοῦ τοῦ ἀνθρώπου και
Amane, amane lego humin, ean may **phagete** tane **sarka** tou huiou tou anthropou kai

` πίητε αὐτοῦ τὸ αἷμα, οὐκ ἔχετε ζωὴν ἐν ἑαυτοῖς. ὁ **τρώγων** μου τὴν **σάρκα** και
pinte autou to aima, ouk ekete zoan en eautois. Ho **trogoan** mou tane sarka kai

` πίνων μου τὸ αἷμα ἔχει ζωὴν αἰώνιον, καγὼ ἀναστήσω αὐτὸν τῇ ἐσχάτῃ ἡμέρᾳ.
pinon mou to aima ekei zoan aionion kago anastaiso auton ta eskata haymera.

ἡ γὰρ **σάρξ** μου **ἀληθής** ἐστιν βρῶσις, καὶ τὸ αἷμα μου **ἀληθής** ἐστιν πόσις. [56]ὁ
Hay gar **sarx** mou alaythas esti brosis kai to aima mou alaythas estin posis. Ho

τρώγων μου τὴν σάρκα καὶ πίνων μου τὸ αἷμα ἐν ἐμοὶ μένει καγὼ ἐν αὐτῷ.
trogoan mou tain sarka kai pinoan mou to aima en emoi menei kago en auto

In the Greek, there are two words for flesh. The first, soma, means dead flesh like a corpse. The one used here "*sarx*" means living breathing flesh. The word *phagein*, he uses for eat, but changes that word in the second sentence to *trogon*, which means to munch, chew or gnaw. He makes the word more physical to stress meaning. This is the only doctrinal teaching over which disciples left him. Would they have left for a symbol?

Jesus wishes to clarify here, and make no mistake that he is speaking literally. If we read further we discover.... "And many left him." How many of you would ever die for a picture of your child or loved one? No one.[24] But would you give your life for the child? Absolutely. The early Christians would never have given their life for a symbol, but a person, absolutely.

The last issue of doctrine, even if they have no problem with Mary; no problem with our idea of the Eucharist, or even scripture. Confession. Even Catholics *protest* this practice. Imagine

> ...if God did not interfere with them, their passsions might one day leave them, but they would never leave their passions; left to themselves the bigoted merely become more bigoted, the sinful more sinful, the greedy more avaricious, the hateful more cruel. Without the in-breaking of God into our sinfulness, our passions might one day leave us, but we would never leave our passions.[25]

Reconciliation is an act on the part of a sorrowful person; an act that says, I want to reunite myself with You. Jesus never sinned, and yet he offered the *sin offering* every year. If we are to be like Christ, what are we to do?

I offer you these lessons in the faith, in the hope that, having been empowered with such knowledge, we might be able to explain to the *lost* the misunderstandings which precipitated it. I imagine if I asked how many of you never heard these things explained in this manner, that most if not all of you would raise your hands. Being the Good

Shepherd, who will die for the sheep means speaking the truth, in season and out of season, so we may draw even those sheep who do not know they are a part of this fold, into the flock.

---

23 *Quoted from Patrick Madrid in a talk given to the Priests of the Diocese of Harrisburg at the Continuing Education Workshop, Hunt Valley MD. 2006.*
24 *Ibid.*
25 *Fulton Sheen. Lift Up Your Hearts. (New York: McGraw-Hill Book Company, Inc., 1950). 200.*

FIFTH SUNDAY OF EASTER
(CYCLE B)
(ACTS 9:26-31; 1 JOHN 3:18-24; JOHN 15: 1-8)

Seeking out the Lost Part III

This month I've decided to focus on the lost. Those sheep which the Good Shepherd seeks. We came to discover in the first week, the top ten reasons why Catholics leave the faith, and why non-Catholic Christians are reluctant to join the faith. Through this we discovered that there is usually a precipitating factor or reason why they left. Last week, we spoke of two major reasons: disagreement with doctrine, and misunderstandings of the faith. Hopefully in trying to illuminate the five doctrines, those who have left or are misunderstanding the faith might have a better grasp of what it means to be part of the Holy Roman Catholic Church.

So what do we talk about this week. Of those ten reasons, I decided I might focus on those *non-Christian* faiths that often draw Catholics to their temples and the reasons they seem so appealing to one who is **not being fed**. Of the major religions of the world, a few Catholics will at one time or another be drawn to Islam, Buddhism, or Hinduism.

So with all of these to choose from, we need to ask ourselves a fundamental question. Are you ready?....How do we know OUR faith is the real faith? That's the million dollar question. How do we know? "And his commandment is this: we should believe in the name of his Son, Jesus Christ, and love one another just as he commanded us. Those who keep his commandments remain in him, and he in them, and the way we know that he remains in us is from the Spirit that he gave us." So let's take a look at each of these traditions and see what THEY offer that our Catholic Faith does not.

God Made Man:

Mohammed never claimed to be a god. In fact it was almost two centuries after Mohammed that a divine mythology ensued. It took that long. The Koran was allegedly written by a Byzantine priest. Mohammed, like Elijah, was said to have been assumed into heaven.

Buddha said that he should not be the focus of any disciples. His teaching should be the focus. He didn't even want disciples, so much as he wanted to reach *Nirvana* for himself. No divine nature was ascribed him until centuries after his death. Death from indigestion.

Hindus have the best of both worlds. Although they can believe in over three hundred million gods, they believe in a high god, and then lesser deities. But their god would never become a man.

Why is it important that God became man? Salvation. One cannot save what one has not assumed.

Salvation:

Allah will overlook the bad if one does enough good deeds. Now, although this is not perfect justice (they can bargain and seal their own salvation) they try to earn paradise. How do they do this? They pray, they pilgrimage and fast and defend the faith. So how much will it take to overshadow the bad they have done? Never enough. They cannot control God.

Buddhists claim that we are all living in an illusion, and that you and I; space and time; matter and soul are all illusions. That's fine to believe, but it doesn't make it true. We can never know how much effort (something we do) it will take to reach *Nirvana*.

Hindus never know how many lifetimes it may take to work out *Karma*. Again, something we can do over many lifetimes. So one can never help another out of a bad place, lest they mess up another's destiny.

What do these traditions have that draw so many in…and what don't they have?

Many are attracted to Buddhism and Hinduism because of the focus, meditation and devotion to betterment of self. Ever hear of contemplation? The divine meditations? Ignatian exercises? Ever hear of the images of our Lady; theophanies of the saints? Ever hear how Christ prayed all night long?

They admire the fasting and ascetic exercises of the Hindus and Muslims. Ever hear of abstaining from meat on Fridays; fasting and giving alms. Have you ever considered making a holy hour or hours; attending daily Mass?

They admire the Buddhist's purging of the spirit and the Muslims devotion to praying daily twice a day. Have you ever considered confession? How about Morning and Evening prayer of the Liturgy of the Hours (the official prayer of the Church)?

They talk about leaders who prayed all day long, went away to be by themselves in order to find *their* way to salvation. Have you ever heard of Christ, who gave himself to death, for which he was innocent, so that *others* might live. Christ, who was the light, and was called the Son of God, not two centuries after his death; not one century after his death, <u>but during his lifetime</u>. The same Jesus who performed miracles (not Mohammed or Buddha), who was tortured for his teaching and died for others. Could anyone ask for more?

Why is it then that we even consider drawing away from the one we know is our only hope of salvation? Because we feel we are not being fed. Part of the problem is that we live in a world of instant gratification in entertainment. Worship means giving of ourselves completely to the One who gave to us as much. It means offering our time in prayer and song and focus to the one who gave us breath this morning, in the way that is the *best we* can offer. To be fed, one has to eat. If we don't eat...we die. *"Just as a branch cannot bear fruit on its own unless it remains on the vine, so neither can you unless you remain in me. I am the vine, you are the branches. Whoever remains in me and I in him will bear much fruit, because without me you can do nothing."*

Some people are being fed...however, one can eat the same food every day and they are being fed, but they can easily lose their appetite. The Liturgy is not some torture that is pressed upon us in an effort to make us feel like we are sacrificing. It is a prayer that is to draw us deeper into the mystery of our God. This is a constant work for us...both those who attend the Liturgy and those who plan it. We need to continue to work to reach the people where they are in their spiritual journey, while also exhorting them to offer everything they have in worship. This is not only the responsibility of the Liturgy, but of the people. It requires a mind and heart that is focused on other and the worship of God MORE, and focused on what THEY GET OUT of IT, less. When we do that...then we have begun to understand the great mysticism that our faith offers; the opportunities for growth and sanctification. Even Ghandi once said: "I would be a Christian in an instant...if Christians but followed the teachings of Christ."

SIXTH SUNDAY OF EASTER
(CYCLE B)
(ACTS 10:25-26, 34-35, 44-48; 1 JOHN 4:7-10; 15:9-17)

Seeking out the Lost Part IV

This month we've decided to focus on the lost. Those sheep which the Good Shepherd seeks. We have come to discover in the first week, the top ten reasons why Catholics leave the faith, and why non-Catholic Christians are reluctant to join the faith. Through this we discover that there is usually a precipitating factor or reason why they left. Last week, we spoke about the major non-Christian religions that draw Catholics away from the faith, and the necessity of worship because of the truths we come to discover are the reality.

There are many moral issues that arise in our faith. Many of them, we have in common with the other Christian and non-Christian faiths as well. However, there are some major differences which will draw Catholics away from their true faith to the Protestant tradition, or which will keep non-Catholics from joining our faith. Although Euthanasia and the Death Penalty are hot topics right now, these are not reasons people typically leave the Church. Even though cloning and abortion weigh high on our scale of justice; we are in agreement with most non-Catholic traditions. Even in our social justice, we are often revered for all we do in the world and work hand-in-hand with the other traditions. So what are the issues? I have found in my experience that there are four major ethical issues that are sometimes the precipitant event for someone to leave the faith.

The first, and greatest of these is marriage and divorce. Therefore, I want to explain what the Church teaches about the Sacrament of Marriage and why it seems so difficult to get married in the Church. We know the statistics. We know there are prenuptial agreements; we know there are separate accounts, etc. That is the difference between a sacrament and being outside of the Sacrament. A Sacrament occurs outside of space and time, and therefore although we can see the symbols; although we can experience the grace, we cannot touch the Sacrament. That is why marriage, if valid, is a perpetual bond here on earth as long as the spouses are alive. It is not merely a contract, but a covenant. So great is the gift that God allows those married to share in His creative act.

When I interview a couple before marriage there are always two questions I ask. The first is…how do you fight? And if they say "We don't," then I start one. Sometimes one can be in such a hurry to get married that they don't think about the marriage. The second question: what is the absolute worst thing that could happen in your marriage, short of death? You are taking them for better or worse…that is the worst. What about when Jesus says "Except in the case of adultery" (*Mt. 19:9*)? The word in the Gospel in the original Greek is *porneia*, which in Greek means "incest." If someone is related to another, they cannot validly marry them. Therefore, Jesus said divorce is permitted because they are not married in the first place. So what is annulment? No such thing. There is a decree of nullity. This means that there was never an unbreakable sacrament. If you are not married in the Church, then it would be good to get married in the Church. If you're going to build the house you can do it in two ways: with tools or without… which would you choose.

Many will leave the Church because they are divorced and remarried, and other faith traditions will allow this. We can pluck our eyes out so we no longer see what is reality, but reality still exists. Ask Jesus how it was from the beginning. He says in the Gospel: *Remain in my love…if you keep my commandments you will remain in my love.* This is freedom, but we have a mistaken understanding of freedom. That brings us to the second topic: Homosexuality.

I would like to read to you from a document from the Bishops Committee on Marriage and the Family: *"Always our Children."*

There seems to be no single cause of a homosexual orientation. A common opinion of experts is that there are multiple factors—

genetic, hormonal, psychological—that may give rise to it. Generally, homosexual orientation is <u>experienced as a given, not as something freely chosen. By itself, therefore, a homosexual orientation cannot be considered sinful, for morality presumes the freedom to choose.</u>

All in all, it is essential to recall one basic truth. <u>God loves every person as a unique individual.</u> Sexual identity helps to define the unique persons we are, and one component of our sexual identity is sexual orientation. <u>Thus, our total personhood is more encompassing than sexual orientation. "Human beings see the appearance, but the Lord looks into the heart"</u> (cf. 1 Sm 16:7).

It is not sufficient only to avoid unjust discrimination. Homosexual persons "must be accepted with respect, compassion and sensitivity"[26]

As a pop culture, we tend to accept the laws that society dictates by lifestyle. We accept their arguments, when we know the truth. The committee here does not shy away from the truth, but in their conviction they also show love. When these souls approached Jesus, I know that he would never have condemned them. He says time and time again, *I have not come into the world to condemn the world, but so that the world might have life, and have it abundantly.* But he also <u>never accepted sin out of pastoral compassion.</u> He would never have justified an act that is *ordered against* the purpose of our sexuality, but he would never reject the person who suffered through it either. Churches that accept this act as acceptable are not teaching the truth of Christ. But a Church that alienates these people and does not show them love, also does not know the teaching of Christ.

Listen to Peter: *God shows no partiality. Rather in every nation whoever fears Him and acts uprightly is acceptable to Him.* We speak the truth, we condemn the sin, but we must love the sinner, and struggle with them to follow the will of God.

These last two reasons are clumped together because while one issue has to do with preventing life, the other has to do with causing life. I place these two last because they are the "secret sins." The other two issues are more or less public, or can be, while these seem to be kept private or only spoken of in certain circles. The first is contraception, the second is *in vitro* fertilization. Granted, people don't always leave the church for these reasons, because they're practiced in secret, but I assure you, these practices are gravely sinful, and if I didn't tell you that, I would be responsible for that sin.

> *If I say to the wicked, 'You shall surely die,' and you give him no warning, nor speak to warn the wicked from his wicked way, in order to save his life, that wicked man shall die in his iniquity; but his blood I will require at your hand. But if you warn the wicked, and he does not turn from his wickedness, or from his wicked way, he shall die in his iniquity; but you will have saved your life.* (Ezekial: 3:18)

God offers us this powerful gift to share in His creative act, and because we do not trust, we reject that gift. We accept pleasure as an end in itself instead of a side effect of the great gift our Lord has entrusted to us. We objectify each other. Where is the sacrifice there? "Love one another as I love you…No one has greater love than this, to lay down one's life for one's friends" (*John 15: 12-13*). Sacrifice.

In the same respect we sometimes forget that this is a gift….not a right. In *in vitro* fertilization (IVF), many people are unaware that the process will kill various other embryos in favor of the one that might survive. And I know this is difficult, as my sister in her own life has had countless problems conceiving, and yet when she found out about the process, and how many persons are killed, etc. to get pregnant, she would not ever have considered it unless she took all pregnancies to term.

You can go to many other Churches and they will accept all of these practices without question. What seems ironic to me, however, is up until the 20th century, all churches were united in these issues; all were non-issues. When did the truth change? Let us ask ourselves how much the popular culture influences our decisions. If we abide in Christ He will abide with us. Unfortunately, there is sometimes no chance to work through these issues and pray through them, because at the time, or shortly thereafter, we are suffering from an apathy. Just not caring enough about spiritual health to do anything. Next week, I will close with this last issue of apathy and give some strategies through which we can reclaim the lost.

---

26 *Always Our Children: A Pastoral Message to Parents of Homosexual Children and Suggestions for Pastoral Ministers. A Statement of the Bishops' Committee on Marriage and Family.*

SEVENTH SUNDAY OF EASTER
(CYCLE B)
(ACTS 1: 15-17, 20A, 20C-26; 1 JOHN 4:11-16; JOHN 17:11B-19)

Seeking out the Lost Part V

This month I've decided to focus on the lost. Those sheep which the Good Shepherd seeks. We have come to discover in the first week, the top ten reasons why Catholics leave the faith, and why non-Catholic Christians are reluctant to join the faith. Through this we discover that there is usually a precipitating factor or reason why they left. The final reasons I want to discuss briefly are **family, apathy and scandal**.

One of the reasons Catholics fall away from the faith, or non-Catholics are resistant to entering the faith has to do with their **family**. Sometimes it is a matter of converting that would cause hostility in the family situation for non-Catholics. However, for Catholics, it is often the opposite. Sometimes we have insured that individuals will either fall away from the faith or certainly never return. This is difficult, especially for parents, because you see it as your charge to have the children come to Mass. And we should train them early on to do that. We take them to school and they may not like it...to practices and they may not like it, and yet for some reason, Mass becomes optional. They must see that WE value it, and then they will too. It does not mean they will want to go, but they WILL go.

Often, however, I think the opposite occurs as well. We nag and beg and plead them so much, that they will never go again. It will take some tolerance and creativity on our part. You can only do the best you can. At least if you cannot get them to Church continue to give good example. This good example is often the influence that gets them back in the pews.

Sometimes, this unwillingness to practice the faith is simply **apathy**. Make no mistake, our Lord accepts failure, if we're trying to be faithful, but He does not accept apathy. This apathy is manifested when people just don't feel anything about the faith, they don't feel in touch with the Spirit. This can be due to a hopeless situation they're in…because they feel God has abandoned them, etc. Usually it will take some great crisis to snap them out of this, but it's never 100%. I must tell you that after last week's homily, I received over twenty-five emails and letters commenting, sometimes negatively, on what I said. This was great! For many reasons. First…it gave me more material for homilies; secondly, it showed people are listening! No one likes to be told to change or to feel as though they have to change, because that points to imperfection. "If I said something wrong, then tell me what it was…but if I spoke the truth, why do you strike me" (*John 18:23*)?

One of the major reasons I thought the comments were so great, is that people took time and really put their hearts into their concerns… they cared! Just to bring two particular letters to mind. The first, when I was speaking about couples who were trying to have children using fertility methods, a couple pointed out that I focused on "creating children" as a purpose of marriage, but never on "parenting children." That for some, "creating children" is not an option, and in speaking on that I totally neglected adoption. If you were outside of my office door you could've heard an audible gasp. They were absolutely right! I'm going to get a hold of them so I can use parts of their letter, because their theology of marriage and the creation was excellent. Mind you, there's no malice there, but I needed to know that. This goes back to the family…that to create a child isn't simply a physical act, but a movement that begins with conception and ends at their death. That in creating life, we form the child until their death. For even when we die, we continue to help them toward that goal of their salvation. What a powerful statement.

The second letter was written by a couple who had been away from the Church for two years. And essentially what they wrote is that they remembered last week why they left. It wasn't any of the issues about which I spoke, it was (in their words) the inability of Catholics to take their Sunday Piousness outside of the Church. This is a valid concern and leads to the last reason I will speak of today. Scandal.

I said the first week that scandal is like spiritual murder. This is not only on the clerical level, where we know the scandal that has purged the Church of many bad elements over the last few years, and is now purging the schools and other institutions. We can see that, because it's all over the papers. I'm speaking of the subtle scandal we expose the people to, around us. This individual brought some of these scandalous actions to my attention in their letter.

That one might offer you the sign of peace and then almost run you over in the parking lot trying to escape before traffic begins; that many Catholics become notorious gossips or cause other scandal by their actions outside of the Church. That many who pray fervently and are devout will cast an angry look at a child who cries during Mass, or will be impatient with those who have families or children.

What is true is that we all have to work on living this life. One can come to church every Sunday and still be apathetic. They come here and do not allow for the Spirit to touch them, but simply come so they will not go to Hell. That is an apathy as well, and very subtly gives scandal. These letters, among others show what it is to be a part of something bigger than themselves; to be Church. It is not enough to benignly sit in the pew and listen to the word, without allowing the Word to become a part of us. When we can allow this experience to change us, then it can change those around us....it becomes the lens through which we view everything else.

I would like to conclude with 10 mistakes Catholics make in bringing back to the faith those who have strayed.

10 mistakes Catholics make[27]
1. They don't share the faith and this is usually a manifestation of apathy
2. Not sharing the *whole* faith: only what is comfortable: Mary, not morals, etc.
3. Evangelize for the wrong reasons: numbers, to be right, etc.
4. Not preparing through study: this leads to misunderstandings

and shutting off

5. Not preparing through prayer
6. Not assessing the situation
7. More Catholic than the Pope
8. Not listening to the people they are evangelizing. Everyone has a story.
9. Worry about Bible verse memorization
10. Forgetting that conversion is the work of the Holy Spirit

And so how do we reclaim the lost? How would Jesus do that with a sheep? Would he beat the sheep? Starve it, so it would not run away again? Would he cage it up in a bin and let it remain there to think about what it did? Or would he take it in his arms, lift it up on his shoulders and carry it back to the flock?

---

27 *Quoted from Patrick Madrid in a talk given to the Priests of the Diocese of Harrisburg at the Continuing Education Workshop, Hunt Valley MD, 2006.*

ASCENSION THURSDAY
(CYCLE B)
(ACTS 1:1-11; EPHESIANS 1:17-23; MARK 16:15-20)

…it would be an ascension…

What if today were your last day? It has happened to me sometimes where people will approach and say: "Father…the Doctor gives me three weeks." What if today were your last day? You've lived for what seems like a short moment, and then (turned all the lights out at this point…all the lights) darkness….night forever. That is (light begins to come up) unless we believe in something more. And if in fact we do believe in something more; then the fact that today is your last day wouldn't matter; unless you were living for "this" life. "He wanted to stay…but he had to go."[28]

Did you feel the coldness of that dark? Did you feel alone… unsettled. For some, that is real; for some, that's all there is. Why would anyone want to live for tomorrow, if that's ultimately what we have to look forward to? For this reason, the Ascension is so important to us! Because it proves to us that there is so much more.

I want you to imagine for a minute…really imagine: This *IS* your last day. Did you do all you wanted to? Make all the money you wanted to? Bought all you wanted? Loved all you wanted? Experienced all you wanted? No? NO! You can't possibly, even if you were to live a thousand years. Because we were not made for this world, but for the next. We can't do all we want to do? Buy all we want, experience everything…but love…can we die today saying we loved all we could? Could we leave this world behind this day, knowing that we were good? I'm not talking good, being good, etc. I'm talking about goodness; would our Creator know *our* voice, *our* face, *our* effect in the world?

We don't have to believe in God in order for Him to exist; anymore than we don't have to believe in bacteria, in order to die of pneumonia. We can deny we have a relationship with Him, but that

IS our relationship with Him. We can pretend that this world *IS*, all there is; but the act must end sometime. You see, to live for God…to live for the next life does not mean that we forget this one; it does not mean that we deny the real things happening now and the impact of those things, not at all. What it means is that we are *IN* the world, but not *OF* the world. It means that we are detached from the "things" in this life in such a way that our happiness does not depend on them; THAT is freedom; anything else is simply an illusion.

Paul writes to the Ephesians: "May the eyes of your hearts be enlightened, that you may know what is the hope that belongs to his call, what are the riches of his glory in his inheritance…and what is the surpassing greatness of his power." This enlightened heart can see beyond the walls of this world to the one we were created for.

How do we obtain this "enlightenment"? Christ showed us how, but it must be real…not just pretty words; not as Br. Elliott Maloney would say, "sky language". It means a different existence where our happiness is no more dependent on things which will never be enough; our happiness is not dependent on what people say about us, so much as who we ARE. It is the only way Christ ever could have experienced so many deaths before his actual crucifixion. It's the only way he could have left them again, after the resurrection. That we live for the only One who can satisfy our longing.

Ronald Rolheiser gives an image which I think truly gives food for thought. He writes:

Imagine if you could speak to the baby in the womb before it was born. Having never seen the light of this world, knowing only the confines and comfort and warmth of the womb, the baby would, I suspect be pretty skeptical about the existence of a world beyond that womb. In fact, if we could speak to that child, we might have quite a difficult time convincing the child that the world outside is much bigger and that it would be in their best interest to be born. If the baby *were* conscious, it would have to make a real act of faith, to believe in life after birth. It would have to have a great hope, in order to make that step.[29]

And so it is with us. In the past, the saints called the day of their death, their *dies natalis*, or "birthday." But only one who has hope in something beyond this world... can anticipate such a birth.

Imagine this were your last day. But imagine a last day, having lived for the One to whom you were returning; imagine a last day when you can have honestly said, you loved...I mean really loved. Imagine a last day where you were detached from the things of this world in a way that you were truly free. A last day (which can come at any moment) for such a person would not nearly be considered a failure, as the world would have us believe...a moment...and then forever night... NO... such a day; for such a person; we would call, by a special name. We would call that, an Ascension!

---

28 *Bishop Nicholas Dattilo, DD., From a homily given on the Feast of the Ascension of our Lord, 2001.*
29 *Based on a quote from: Fr. Ronald Rolheiser, OMI., Against the Infinite Horizon: The Finger of God in Our Everyday Lives, (New York: The Crossroad Publishing Company, 2001), 116.*

PENTECOST SUNDAY
(CYCLE B)
(ACTS 2: 1-11; 1 CORINTHIANS 12:3B-7, 12-13; JOHN 20:19-23)

The gift that one can never give oneself

Have you ever met someone who has everything. You want to buy them a gift, or do something nice for them, but it is next to impossible. My brother is like that sometimes. I see a new gadget or something and think: "Oh he'll love this." and when I go to purchase it he has it already. You want to give them a gift, but they have it all…how do you give to someone like that?

Wouldn't you think that the greatest satisfaction is giving a gift to someone who could never possibly attain that gift themselves. For instance, like these programs for those with terminal illness: "Make a wish Foundation" or these ranches or camps which take kids out into nature and allow them to experience things that otherwise might be impossible. Imagine being able to give a gift to someone who can never pay you back; who will never be able to do anything comparable for you in the future. Imagine giving the gift that they cannot provide for themselves, and you will remember the "ahh" you once had roll from your lips on Christmas or your Birthday. The wonderful satisfaction that is received when "We've done good." That feeling, much as we see in Acts, that crosses cultural boundaries, languages, and sexes. Something that is innate but understood by all.

Sometimes, the simplest gifts given from heart far outweigh anything we could buy. What could we possible offer to someone who has everything? How about peace; Forgiveness; A listening ear; Some time spent? "There are different kinds of spiritual gifts but the same Spirit." But what about gifts to us? How much would we appreciate a gift given to us, that we could not obtain for ourselves, regardless of how much we tried, or who we asked? This is the gift we celebrate today; this type of gift comes to us…from the Holy Spirit. But it requires that we first empty ourselves; dry ourselves out.

The apostles are at the end of their rope. They are holed up in the room with Mary the mother of Jesus. They are now empty vessels; Jesus has departed. They are like dry pieces of tinder…the perfect conditions for a fire. The doors open and they are filled with the breath of the Spirit…but that could only happen because they were first empty. They then received tongues of fire; and a Church was born…our Church. And an inferno was ignited in their hearts; a fire that is not diminished because it is dispersed; "a fire divided but undimmed."

The apostles who had no real skills to speak of theologically…they who had nothing to give seemingly; and yet they emptied themselves and were filled. A gift they could not provide for themselves. We see in these individuals what can happen when we have the wind around us… the fire of the Holy Spirit, and the dust from which we are created.

(I then threw up a fine powder amidst a flame and an enormous flame erupted.)

A PENTECOST!

TRINITY SUNDAY
(CYCLE B)
(DEUTERONOMY 4:32-34, 39-40; ROMANS 8:14-17; MATTHEW 28:16-20)

The Divine Relationship

Have you ever talked to yourself? Well?.....if you answered "no" you just did! Why do we do it? My mom used to talk to herself all the time....she admitted it. We'd be bad and she'd be yelling at the top of her lungs at us, and then she'd say time and time again: "It's like talking to myself." Why do we do it?

There was a movie out a few years ago, called "Castaway". I'm not going to give away the ending but Tom Hanks is stranded on an island because of a crash. He is there alone and all he has with him is some items salvaged from the wreck. One of the things is a volleyball, he names "Wilson" for obvious reasons. And for some time, he grows very attached to it...even speaking to it. Why would anyone ever do that? Ask someone who's been in solitary confinement, within a prison camp or otherwise.

There was a study done on infants in an orphanage. They had all been fed and nourished, given water and bedding, but those who were never held died. Human touch.... Contact with another is part of who we are, and because they did not have that...they died. Why should this surprise us? We were created by a perfect union of persons, in a perfect relationship.

"The Father pours fourth everything He is into the Son who returns all that he has to the Father. And that love between them is so strong that it manifests itself as a presence we call the Holy Spirit. This is the 'Divine Drama'"[30]. This Trinity has been described by some ancient writers as a dance between two lovers. The Father and Son embrace in a dance which is the Holy Spirit.

We, are the first Trinitarian miracle, called toward this perfect union with God, and with the presence of God in each other. The Father gave us our form from the dust of the earth, but knew that earthly nourishment would not satisfy our hunger and so He made the ultimate sacrifice in His son; that he might nourish us eternally. But even with nourishment, one cannot live without breath. So he offers His Spirit who fills our souls.

Our attempt to connect with another is our innate desire to return to the Divine. There is a theologian who once commented on this longing. He said:

When God created the human heart, he found it so good, and so loving, that He took a small piece of it and kept it with Him in heaven. That's why our heart is not the shape of a valentine heart. Therefore in this life, we can we can never love anything whole-heartedly; because we have not a whole heart with which to love. But we are drawn to something beyond this world, so that when we finally return to our Creator, we can reclaim that piece of our heart that was kept safe from the beginning.[31]

This means we will never be alone. The Father has been there from the very beginning, but we were separated, and our ability to love completely was removed by sin. So He sent his Son, and even then some rejected him; but those who stayed with him learned to love, and to see God in other people. Even then, His son would have to leave and when he left, they felt alone…but He didn't leave them without an Advocate. He sent the Spirit and in his last words then, we discover the secret we should have known all along. "I will be with you…always…until the end of the ages."

---

30 *Fr. Justin Matro, OSB. Homily given in St. Gregory Chapel at St. Vincent Seminary, Latrobe PA. 2003.*
31 *Bishop Fulton J Sheen, Preface to Religion in The Angel's Blackboard: The Best of Fulton J. Sheen,*
  (Liguori, Missori: Liguori/Triumph Press, 1995), 123.

Ninth Sunday in Tempus per Annum (Cycle B)
(Deuteronomy 5:12-15; 2 Corinthians 4: 6-11; Mark 2:23-3:6)

Forget the 7ᵗʰ day…how are we living the other Six?

God rested on the seventh day, because He knew if he didn't give us an excuse to take some rest…we would not rest. Some might doubt, and yet we live in a world of individuals who appear to be "living to work" as opposed to "working in order to live." Deuteronomy gives four specific recommendations of how to fulfill this law. We might ask why they had to be so detailed. And yet all we need to do is look at our human condition and the answer is clear. Because even when told directly to "take it easy" and even when God himself rested, we still find excuses or loopholes through which we might pass, "just to get this little bit done."

Part of the difficulty is that we are doing our "own" work. We are about the work that we "have" to do or think we must do. The fact is this: People run around like chickens with their heads cut off trying to do everything under the sun, and we will never have enough time to do all the things we want to do. We will always have enough time to do those things we are supposed to do. This Sabbath rest doesn't simply rely on the fact that we work for six days and rest on the seventh; it relies on the fact that the six days we do work, the work is the work of God.

A man approached a holy priest with whom he had sought direction over time. "I believe I have finally reached the highest level of sanctity." The priest replied: "What makes you think you have reached that point?" The man said: "I fast all day, every day; when I am tempted I flagellate myself with a leather whip; and don't take so much time to clean and look at my appearance; and I work day after day without complaint." The priest looked out the window and called the man over. "See that horse out there? Day after day it remains tied to that stake. It is rarely fed and is beaten mercilessly by its owner. It works all day long without a break and I will see it on occasion rolling in the dirt. Now I ask you: Is that a saint or a horse?"[32]

The issue Jesus has with the Pharisees is this: they are so concerned about the people resting on the seventh day to follow the law, that they are unconcerned with their lack of charity the other six days. Give the Pharisees some credit, they were dealing with a stiff-necked people (we don't know any of them) who were trying to work themselves to death, so the Pharisees are responding to that mentality. In the same respect, however, we see clearly the point Jesus is making by the question. "Is it lawful to do good on the Sabbath rather than do evil, to save life rather than to destroy it?" They remained silent. See there is more to being a witness; to being a saint, than simply following a law. Anyone can do as much, but it doesn't make them a saint. A horse maybe…but not a saint!

---

32 Based on story told by Rev. Ronald Rolheiser, OMI, *The Shattered Lantern: Rediscovering a Felt Presence of God,* (New York: The Crossroad Publishing Company, 2001), 179-180.

TENTH SUNDAY IN TEMPUS PER ANNUM (CYCLE B)
(GENESIS 3:9-15; 2 CORINTHIANS 4:13-5:1; MARK 3:20-35)

*Sin must be momentary insanity;
if it's not, then it just doesn't make sense.*

Sin is a crazy thing. Why would anyone commit a sin? Let's face it, would anyone want to separate themselves from true beauty? True goodness? True light? Of course not. So why do we choose sin? "Because it's delicious," as one of my Theology professors used to say. What is delicious? Tasty. But tasty doesn't mean good necessarily. Candy is tasty until it means a cavity; french fries are tasty until they mean a heart attack; sushi is tasty, until it means *trichinosis*. We do not want to be separated from God but then we choose something *seemingly* better. We choose the *created* over the *Creator*.

There was a time though, you know, when sin was not. In fact, we didn't even know we could sin. All was right in the world so to speak. We had everything we needed. Need was the important thing, but we had not yet discovered "want." Want is different from need. Want is a result of original sin; the original sin of the angels who were banished into a grotesque ugliness called hell. Want is the grasping for something we were never meant to have. If we were meant to have it, then it wouldn't be want; it would be need. "The Lord is my shepherd, I shall not *want*."[33] And our *Needs are* met.

So we never knew what it was *to want* in the beginning. We had everything we needed. We could've gone on like that forever; *we would've* gone on like that forever, unless someone or something introduced "want" to us. It's so fascinating to me that some of the poorest people I've met, don't know they're poor. And then Mother Theresa came out with this quote which I think sums it up. "The

97

rich are not those who have everything; the rich are those who need nothing."

To *Need nothing*. That was the state of things. Adam and Eve had it all. They needed nothing. But then another had to intervene and introduce "want." The desire within us that can never be satisfied because it was never meant to be there. He introduced *want* to Eve; who introduced want or desire to the man; and it has been there ever since. A baby doesn't cry for want...but for need. At least until that child is introduced to "have" and then it "wants." Such was the case for these new creatures. Bliss was not enough. Desire for more drives many through life and yet possession never satisfies that hunger but only aggravates it.

Want focuses on what one does not possess. Desire focuses on what one lacks. Both of these drive us to cling to that which we have no right to possess. How do we know this? Because once we possess it; that which fills not a need; we crave something else. Such was the case when the *diabolos* or tempter entered the garden. He would enter the garden again in the first century to try and tempt the One who was present at his very inception. Sin is a moment of temporary insanity; but a moment that has repercussions throughout time and space and beyond. We observe the blackness and cold ugliness that was a result of one sin of pride among celestial beings. Now witness millions of voices crying out in absolute solitude and misery and you have heard the effect of sin on God. That we repeat a million times a minute is the sin of those original creatures before God their maker. We commit the original sin of the desire *to be Him*. The tears of God are made up of the sins of His creatures in their moments of insanity. And when we think of all we have; when we think of the One who gave it to us, then sin really would have to be a moment of insanity, wouldn't it? Because who would ever turn away from such a One? If it's not insanity, then what are we doing?! "Father forgive them...the know not what they are doing" (*Luke 23:34*).

---

33 *Revised Standard Version, Psalm 23.*

Eleventh Sunday in Tempus per Annum (Cycle B)
(Ezekial 17:22-6-24; 2 Corinthians 5:6-10; Mark 4:26-34)

Bloom where you're planted...or transplanted.

Having been up in the woods and cutting down trees I have rarely thought about the history these *old men* have. One day it was raining and I sat on the porch out of the rain and was staring off into space. We had cut down an oak and it was laying there in the soil, with the rain dropping down and splitting into pieces while what soaked in ran in rivulets down the bark. If you've ever examined an oak, you know the bark is not flat and looks as if someone took individual pieces of bark the size of cigars and pasted them up and down the tree. I began to think about all that this tree has seen. The long history of this tree, probably at least one-hundred years old. And here it is dead. And yet, how many more oaks has it given life to over the last hundred years?

The *Cedars of Lebanon* were legendary. They are spoken of in the psalms and alluded to by the prophets and yet through the prophet Ezekial, God speaks of tearing off a tender shoot from the top and of planting this shoot which will form another tree. And because this has been transplanted, it leaves the rest of the tree behind. The years of history behind. It will leave behind the blights, gypsy moths, grubs, fractures, all the impurities that have crept in, and grow anew. A tree cannot do this itself (unless of course an Ent[34]) but it can only be done through the Divine. And so the same is true of us. Jesus talks about the kingdom as a mustard seed. The smallest of seeds, etc., and pretty much useless. It is a "tree-not-yet". But once sown, it becomes the largest of plants. It must be sown, however. Okay, so now what?

Many of us get stuck...we get in a *rut* in life. Perhaps plans didn't turn out the way we had hoped. Perhaps we've messed up along the way. Perhaps we've never really been close with God and so there's pretty much no reason to start at this point. That why Ezekial is preaching to us. Because the first step to reclaiming our lives is not to pick up a self-help book, or watch a motivational speaker at two in the morning. The first step is to invite God into your life. Now here's a gentle warning: If you invite the *pruner* to come for a visit, He will take some off the top! In other words, this will not be a painless process to say the least. And I would dare say, those processes that in the end are best for us, are typically not painless.

So, our Lord will graft from you a bud. All the stuff from the past: the blight, grubs, moths, all those things which drew us away from Him, or separated us from Him or convinced us that He was not...all of that is left behind. And this new plant is absent the impurities and now can start anew. Because it is now free of impurities, we go to the next metaphor which is the mustard seed. That seed is not us, but needs a place in which to be planted. Now free of the impurities, we are not only the plant that has been transplanted and really transformed, but we are the soil. Once open to God, He can sow the seeds of the kingdom, and free from the impurities, we can allow it to grow. All we need to do is want that. So how can we do that? Next week we will consider the ways in which we can detach ourselves from the old way of life...from our trunk so to speak and become that fertile ground for the seeds of the kingdom.

---

34 Ents were the walking and talking trees of the J.R.R. Tolkien series The Lord of the Rings.

Twelfth Sunday in Tempus per Annum (Cycle B)
(Job 38:1, 8-11; 2 Corinthians 5:14-17; Mark 4:35-41)

"For those with faith, life is changed not ended."

A Bible study group was discussing the unforeseen possibility of their sudden death. The leader of the discussion said, "We will all die some day, and none of us really know when, but if we did we would all do a better job of preparing ourselves for that inevitable event." Everybody nodded their heads in agreement with this comment. Then the leader said to the group, "What would you do if you knew you only had four weeks of life remaining before your death, and then the Great Judgment Day?" A gentleman said, "I would go out into my community and minister the Gospel to those that have not yet accepted the Lord into their lives." "Very good!" said the group leader, and all the group members agreed, that would be a very good thing to do.

One lady spoke up and said enthusiastically, "I would dedicate all of my remaining time to serving God, my family, my church, and my fellow man with a greater conviction." "That's wonderful!" the group leader commented, and all the group members agreed, that would be a very good thing to do. But one gentleman in the back finally spoke up loudly and said, "I would go to my mother-in-law's house for the four weeks." Everyone was puzzled by this answer, and the group leader ask, "Why your mother-in-law's home?" Then the gentleman smiled sarcastically and said, "Because, that would make them the longest four weeks of my life!"[35]

We fear death, and the world would see it as the ultimate failure. If you doubt this, look at all the billions that are spent each year preserving us. Last week we were speaking of allowing God to transplant us from our old way of life to the new. That once open to God, He can sow the seeds of the kingdom, and free from the impurities, we can allow it to grow within us. That is a "little death." All we need to do is want that. So how can we do that? "What is it that keeps us from detaching from the things in our lives that are not working, or keeping us away from what is most important?"

> Robert Bellarmine would say:
> Prosperity and adversity, wealth and poverty, health and sickness, honors and humiliations, life and death, in the mind of the wise man, are not sought for their own sake or avoided for their own sake. But, if they contribute to the Glory of God and your eternal happiness, then they are good and should be sought. If they detract from this, then they are evil and should be avoided. [36]

He speaks of things which draw us to God or take from God. We must come to realize that we were not made for this world but for the next. And if we can do that, then we will be able to detach from the unnecessary things of this world to pursue those of the next.

"Teacher, do you not care that we are perishing?" They ask Jesus. Jesus who is asleep amidst a storm. "Why are you terrified?" he responds. He is trying to draw them again and again away from the distractions of this world so that he can focus their hearts on the greater gifts. Paul says it best: "So whoever is in Christ is a new creation: the old things have passed away; behold, new things have come." To realize that we were not created for this world, means it is transitory. If we can set our eyes on the things of the next world, then we will begin to experience "little deaths" with each sacrifice. One of those deaths, then is foregoing our old way of life, for the new life of Christ.

Job says it like none other: "Who shut within doors the sea?" "Who did all these things?" YOU? Anything earthly? NO! It was I who did it. I who hold your world in the palm of my hand. When we come to really believe that, then we realize we're not in control of anything that is truly important in life. We come to rely on the one who created us unlike any others so that He might see us grow and flourish. We are the ones He wishes to free from our past; our past of disease, or blight, or parasites. We are the ones He wishes harbor the seeds of the kingdom. "There will come a time when you believe that everything is finished…that will be the beginning."[37]

35 *Internet Forward*

36 *Saint Robert Bellarmine, "Treatise on the Ascent of the Mind to God", in The Liturgy of the Hours: According to the Roman Rite, volume IV, (New York: Catholic Book Publishing Co., 1975), page 1412.*

37 *Louis L'Amore: Lonely on the Mountain, (Bantam books, 1984).*

THIRTEENTH SUNDAY, TEMPUS PER ANNUM (CYCLE B)
(WISDOM 1:13-15; 2:23-24; 2 CORINTHIANS 8:7,9, 13-15; MARK 5:21-43)

Reconciliation is the completion of Love.

We were never meant for death; but if we choose death, there is nothing our Lord will do to prevent it. We often comment that nothing is impossible for God. However, God cannot contradict Himself. Because we have free will, we can choose against what He desires, and because He gave us free will, He will not change it. But we are never meant to choose death…choose life.

There are two stories brought together in the Gospel. The most unlikely person, the official; he is one of the ones who were persecuting Jesus: this character comes forward, at the end of his rope, asking in desperation for a cure. His daughter is ill, and on the verge of death. Yet another opportunity for God to preserve life. His travel to help this girl is interrupted by another encounter.

Here is a woman who has bled for years, and used everything she had for medical science to find a cure. Here is one who is considered unclean by the community; an unclean person could not interact with others; go to the synagogue, etc. and therefore, she was essential "dead." But she did not choose death. She sought life from the world, and they offered her only death…and then she met Jesus, and everything changed. She was at the bottom, she couldn't possibly get lower and so she took a chance and touched the garment, and they both felt the change.

Jesus arrives at the house only to find the mourners already there. The girl is dead and all hope is lost. But Jesus is the *Lord of Life*. God's Spirit is in the blood and just as He stopped the flow of blood from the woman on the way, he now commands the blood to flow once again in this little one. Both sought the Lord in their death and he raised them up.

Can you imagine one who would not seek life? I can. Another at the end of his rope. Another with blood, but the blood of the Christ on his hands. This other is Judas. One who could not escape from his sin. He allowed the sin to force him into the blackness of despair and because of that, he chose death. What if…another scenario? Benedict Groeshel gives another possible scenario.

What if a few moments before Christ finally expired….breathing maybe once a minute, out of the darkness emerges this character on his knees. His face is cut; his eyes swollen from tears; a rope burn around his neck. He crawls up to the crucified one and asks forgiveness! I guarantee you there would be churches all over the world erected to "St. Judas the Penitent"! There would be so many artists' renditions of that final moment, that one would adorn every church.[38]

Think about how the world might be changed, when one chose life, even in his seeming death. Archeologists have found vials in the tombs and pyramids in Egypt. These vials demonstrated that the Egyptians saved tears.[39] Tears! In order to remember their past suffering, they saved them, so that they would have a constant reminder of those times. Where were these found? In the tombs….in places of death where they belong. We DO the SAME today. Many of us would say we never would choose death and yet we've been saving tears for ages. We cannot get past certain sins because we begin to fall into the same trap that Judas did. We cannot believe that God has the power to forgive our sins. Someone else's, yes, but ours…never! Because of this, we will die a slow terminal death. We can never have life. we will often fall in our sin, and then say, "Well, I've done it once…I've failed, and so doing it more doesn't matter." That is foolishness. A drop of poison can make you sick, a cup of it can kill you. Same poison, different dosage. Don't ever fall into the trap. So how do we choose life?

Touch the hem of the Master. Even in pride, ask the Master for help. One of the symptoms of sin is not to want forgiveness. One of the symptoms of sin is not to want to pray. It's called *Acedia*, and it's a spiritual depression. The first step is to touch the garment of the one who can stop the flow, and the one who can command the life back into us. The moment we sin, we stop and ask forgiveness; make a firm purpose of amendment; and offer a penance; then go to confession.

Jesus stopped preaching that day to raise two people back to life… and that action alone spoke more eloquently than the Sermon on the Mount. Start tonight, right now, and become the person Christ wants you to be…alive…the person you always hoped you could be.

---

38 Fr. Benedict Groeshel CFR, *Arise from Darkness: What to Do When Life Doesn't Make Sense,* (San Francisco, CA: Ignatius Press, 1995), 97-98.
39 Ibid., 92.

Fourteenth Sunday in Tempus per Annum (Cycle B)
(Ezekial 2: 2-5; 2 Corinthians 12:7-10; Mark 6: 1-6)

My grace is sufficient for you

*My grace is sufficient for you....*if you accept it. I want to address two basic concepts today. The first is, what does it mean to be a *prophet*, and secondly, what does it mean to be in *koinonia*? A prophet is one who speaks Christ with actions and words. The prophet is not concerned about acceptance, but accepts all. Their message is not diminished by the attitudes or persecution of the world, but strengthened by it. "My grace is sufficient for you" (*2 Cor. 12:9*). A prophet speaks the truth; not *their* truth, but the truth of God which does not change whether it is accepted or not. The prophet is responsible for revealing this truth to the people but not responsible for their acceptance or denial of it.

Koinonia is a Greek word that is difficult to translate. Some would say, "family" while others "friendship." Perhaps I can give you a glimpse of what it means by an illustration. When the Holy Father, Pope John Paul II visited his home of Poland for the first time, a journalist made this observation. As was his custom, the Pope disembarked from the plane, came forward and kissed the ground. As he approached the people from his home town, they came forward, and one of the elders took his hands, and for just a few moments, looked into each others' eyes. There were no words exchanged, but there was perfect understanding. *That* is *koinonia*.

See, like Paul, do we not all have thorns in our sides? Do we not have those things that plague us time and time again? I was listening to a preacher on the radio one time; his name was Tony Evans. He's a powerful speaker and he relayed a story which I will paraphrase here. There's a woman in the desert who is mortally wounded. Mortally wounded means that if she doesn't receive help, she will probably die. Now, if you know anything about nature, you know when something's about to die, the buzzards begin to circle. That was the case here. The buzzards began to circle in anticipation of an easy meal. Now as an observer, you have two options: You can shoot the buzzards, or remove the person from the desert and heal them. Now, if you shoot the buzzards, they will die; but soon thereafter others will arrive to replace them. But if you remove the person from the desert, and heal them; well then…there will be nothing for the buzzards to feast on, and they'll go away.[40]

We are all in the desert…we are all mortally wounded, but we cannot get out alone. If we try alone, we will fail miserably, but we *must* get out of the desert. Therefore it is up to us to help each other. Why? Because we are in *koinonia*…we are part of the body. Why do support groups work so well? Because everyone there has a common goal: to get rid of the sickness. Is it any wonder that Jesus said: "Wherever two or more are gathered in my name…there am I among them" (*Mt. 18:20*). So when we encounter another we experience that *koinonia*; we understand if even a little. It means we are not alone.

Sometimes, I think of God looking down on His creatures and he sees the fighting and unrest; He sees the murder and poverty, famine and war; he sees the homelessness and hatred and He shouts: "STOP!" Stop! Enough! This is not how it was meant to be…this is not how it was from the beginning.

The buzzards of our world are many, but they are cowards. We must be the prophets and must act counter-culturally; we must preach with our lives and they will know that "a prophet has been in their midst"(*Ezekial 2:5b*). And with our eyes fixed firmly on the Lord, we will look at our neighbors with new eyes and see their gifts we were once blind to. We need to ask ourselves: Am I a prophet with my life, my actions, my gifts? Am I in *koinonia* with those in my parish, working together toward the common goal. As we approach the altar for the highest form of communion let us pray not for our thorns/buzzards to be removed, but that we may accept the grace God gives us through this sacrament and the *koinonia* we share with each other and remove ourselves from the desert.

---

40 Based on a talk given by Dr.. Tony Evans. Radio Spot.

FIFTEENTH SUNDAY IN TEMPUS PER ANNUM (CYCLE B)
(AMOS 7:12 – 15; EPHESIANS 1:3-14; MARK 6:7-13)

I was no prophet, but the Lord took me from the flock and said,
"Go Prophesy."

Amos says: "I was no prophet, nor have I belonged to a company of prophets; I was a shepherd and a dresser of sycamores. The Lord took me from following the flock, and said to me, Go, prophesy to my people Israel." It is not something I would necessarily have chosen for myself. But if we respond to the Creator, who could have made us anybody else…and we accept that purpose for which He has created us, then we will be prophets. Paul says to the Ephesians: "He chose us in him, before the world began…in accord with the favor of his will."

So often we experience God in a way that we haven't before, or think we get a sign, but then begin to second guess. Perhaps what we need is not more signs, but *sight*. The ability to see the signs around us, sometimes in the most subtle ways. It would be unfair of God to give us a purpose and not give us the tools with which to fulfill such a purpose. At the same time, it would be unfair for our Lord to have a purpose for us without us having any way of knowing what that purpose is. What we need is *sight*.

From about third grade on, I pretty much thought I was supposed to be a priest. I used to get up early in the morning and celebrate Mass for my stuffed animals. I even preached, and they made not a single move…they sat most attentively for sometimes thirty minutes. I have since trimmed down the content a bit, but I look on those days as some of the best days. By the time I got to high school, my interests changed a bit. I started dating, and was interested in the sciences. And yet, despite all of that, my vocation was still in the back of my mind.

I decided at sixteen to make a pilgrimage. I didn't even really know what one was at that point and yet I felt it was what I needed to do. I drove to Harrisburg to the cathedral of St. Patrick and spent an hour there. I prayed: "Lord, if you want me to be a priest, then you gotta give me a sign. What is it that you want of me?" And I waited…and waited…and waited. Finally an hour was up and I figured he had His chance, and didn't take it. I had waited for the sign and there was none, so I decided to leave. I could now rest easily. I walked out the doors and the first thing that caught my eye was a billboard. The billboard read: "Need a sign? dial 1-800…." I looked up to the heavens and said: "Gimme another sign."

If someone were to ask me to find a particular hubcap in a junk yard amidst thousands of cars, it would take some time, if I even could find it. If, however, in this particular junkyard there were only three cars, it would be much easier. The fact is that many times we have so many distractions in our lives…so much stuff that is merely no more than filler; so much noise that is not spoken or played; so much clutter that it is difficult to see a hubcap, let alone the junkyard. But if we can clear out the clutter, sometimes what has been hidden for so long, is revealed.

"He instructed them to take nothing for the journey but a walking stick--- no food, no sack, no money in their belts." Take all the normal things we have that surround us and put us into a situation that we are not accustomed to. Take us out of our element and put us into a situation that might be uncomfortable and we cannot depend on ourselves, but perhaps reach beyond ourselves for the first time in our life! That…is sight. When we can have that kind of sight, the veil is lifted and we can see the signs clearly.

When I did eventually decide to enter the seminary, the seeds of doubt were still present, but to a different extent. I had given away or sold most of what I owned in an effort to enter all the way into the experience. My head was clearer, and I could see the signs, and still there was some hesitation.

It was only a month before I was to enter and I was on a trip with my family. We came up through West Virginia and stopped at an Inn. I always had told my mom that I would fall in love with a southern girl…there was just something about that *drawl* that melted me. The hostess was the most charming southern girl I had met and it was all I could do to follow her to our seats without gawking. As we were waiting for our dinner, I walked over to her and we started chatting: I melted when she spoke. But the thought that kept entering my mind was: "This is not a good idea, seeing as how you will be in the seminary in less than a month." Listening to this voice I politely excused myself. As I walked away, however, she called after me and said: "*At least tale me yore name.*"[41] I couldn't believe it! I hadn't even told her my name. I responded: "My name's Mike, what's yours?" And in the sweetest southern drawl she could muster she said, "My name's CHASTITY. This time I looked up to heaven and declared: "YOU win!"

The gift we need is not more and more signs or miracles. The gift we need is sight. Amos had no clue what it meant to be a prophet. He didn't ask for that vocation and probably dreaded it some days. And yet he said yes. Sight necessitates an openness to the One who created it. When we have the faith that allows God to be God, then we will echo the psalmist of psalm 85: "The Lord himself will give his benefits; our land shall yield its increase. Justice shall walk before him, and prepare the way of his steps."

---

41 Spelling to stress the drawl.

Sixteenth Sunday in Tempus per Annum (Cycle B)
(Jeremiah 23: 1-6; Ephesians 2:13-18; Mark 6:30-34)

The Lord is MY Shepherd, I shall want for nothing!

So familiar are we with psalm 23 in the biblical world as well as the secular world that I would be remiss if I didn't discuss it today. I read a book written by a shepherd who comments on this psalm.[42] Not the theology or philosophy but just from what he knows from having shepherded sheep. We often tend to read the psalm as poetry and thus lose some sense of its import as prayer. The psalm begins speaking about the shepherd and ends up by the end, speaking *to* him. I imagine if we believed all that the psalmist writes, we would not so much simply read the psalm, as we would proclaim: "The LORD is MY shepherd...I shall WANT FOR NOTHING! Look at what we have! Thank God.

He is MY shepherd. He owns me not only by the very act of His creating me, but also having purchased me through the blood of His son. Some of us have shepherds, but they are not *Good* shepherds. We have a *Good* Shepherd and so we are earmarked just as a sheep and belong to him. *To want for nothing* implies this contentment. When we sin, it is because we do not trust that God can provide us with what we need. Mother Teresa once said: "The rich are not those who have everything; but those who need nothing." The rest of the psalm is based on the next line: "He gives me repose."

This author speaks of what is necessary for a sheep to lie down, "He gives me repose." In order for a sheep to be comfortable enough to lie down, they cannot be hungry; cannot be experiencing friction with other sheep; cannot be agitated by parasites and must feel safe.

First, if a sheep are hungry, they will forage and be restless. Furthermore, if there is nothing to eat, they will begin to wander. There are those sheep called "fence-crawlers" who will have lush grasses before them and yet will find a way through the fence even if that grass is sub-standard or brown. Often they will put their lives in danger and stray from the shepherd. If they have young lambs, often the lambs will learn to fence crawl beyond the protection of the shepherd and often to their peril.

The second need is to be free of friction with other sheep. If they are fighting with other sheep, or discontent, or males are vying for females, they will be restless. The shepherd will try to dissuade such problems by anointing the horns of the rams with grease. Even modern shepherds today use axle grease. He will place this on their horns and heads so that when they do battle and ram each other, they simply slide off of each other. Typically they can do great damage, but by sliding off of each other in the ram, they can make no progress in the battle and so they give up.

The third need is to be free from flies and parasites. The shepherd will anoint the heads of the sheep with an oil mixture that protects from flies and repels them. The sheep are no longer distracted or debilitated and can rest and will hear the shepherd's voice. He often checks them carefully for parasites under the wool and removes them once they are discovered.

Finally, the sheep must feel safe from predators. Those who are fence crawlers and furthest from the shepherd are most vulnerable to wolves and lions. "Be sober and alert; the devil is prowling like a roaring lion looking for someone to devour. Resist him, solid in your faith" (*1 Peter 5:8-9*). Those sheep who are furthest away....those who have forgotten the sound of the Master's voice are most vulnerable.

When Jesus saw the people he was moved with pity. Like a shepherd he knew each by name, but they had forgotten the voice of their shepherd and so they *seemed* well fed and yet were starving; looking for life-sustaining food, right in front of them and yet they were blind.

They began fighting among themselves for places of honor and jealousy permeated their ranks, and the shepherd would later anoint them with the Holy Spirit. They suffered from distraction, fear, and sinfulness; and he tenderly touched them, and brought their agitation and sin to the surface and healed them through forgiveness. He warned them that not all were sheep but some wolves in sheep's clothing.

We are called to be both sheep and shepherd. We are all called by God to a higher holiness. Jeremiah says very clearly: "I will appoint shepherds to shepherd them and bring them back" or as Paul says: "to those who were once far off…" Those who have been far off for so long they have forgotten the voice of the Good Shepherd, but He has not forgotten them and daily, calls them home. Come home.

---

42 Phillip Keller, *Shepherd looks at Psalm 23, (Grand Rapids, Michigan, 1970), 23, ff.*

Seventeenth Sunday in Tempus per Annum (Cycle B)
(2 Kings 4:42-44; Ephesians 4:1-6; John 6:1-15)

The first requirement of the gift, was that it be given.

The disciples were perplexed. They, who were the adults and seemingly in charge of the crowd could not satisfy their hunger. It would take a little boy ("...you must become like little children" *-Mt. 18:3*) who would offer the meager gift he had, to change history. It would take a little one to offer all he had, so that his generosity would be told in all four Gospels. His generosity is not profiled nearly as much as the miracle, however, I would propose that without him, there might not have been a multiplication.

The Evangelist John is very specific in mentioning that these loaves were barley loaves. Barley loaves were tough and granular and therefore not normally eaten by people. They were the food for pigs and the poor, that's about it. And yet, despite that, this boy offers what little he had (probably to sell) to our Lord. The miracle is not simply that our Lord takes the cheap loaves and makes thousands of them. The real miracle is that once the food has been eaten, "He said to his disciples, 'Gather the fragments left over, so that nothing will be wasted.'" Why collect what normally composed slops for pigs? Because this pig-food or poor man's food, with the blessing of Jesus was not simply multiplied, but transformed.

"Then Jesus took the loaves, gave thanks, and distributed them to the crowd." This bread is now sacred and abundant. The same is true of us. So often we won't offer our true authentic self to God. Either because we fear what might be demanded of us, or because we don't see anything we have as worthy of God's call. The lesson is that what meager offerings we freely give, God can take; bless; and magnify! We need only to let go of all the masks we put up...all the defenses we have constructed over our lifetime in an effort to protect our self and let God do what God does. If we do that, then miracles can happen.

Jenny was a bright-eyed, pretty five-year-old girl. One day when she and her mother were checking out at the grocery store, Jenny saw a plastic pearl necklace priced at $2.50. How she wanted that necklace, and when she asked her mother if she would buy it for her, her mother said, "Well, it is a pretty necklace, but it costs an awful lot of money. I'll tell you what. I'll buy you the necklace, and when we get home we can make up a list of chores that you can do to pay for the necklace. And don't forget that for your birthday Grandma just might give you a whole dollar bill, too. Okay?" Jenny agreed, and her mother bought the pearl necklace for her.

Jenny worked on her chores very hard every day, and sure enough, her Grandma gave her a brand new dollar bill for her birthday. Soon Jenny had paid off the pearls. How Jenny loved those pearls. She wore them everywhere---to kindergarten, to bed and when she went out with her mother to run errands. The only time she didn't wear them was in the shower because her mother had told her that they would turn her neck green! Now Jenny had a very loving daddy. When Jenny went to bed, he would get up from his favorite chair every night and read Jenny her favorite story.

One night when he finished the story, he said, "Jenny, do you love me?" "Oh yes, Daddy, you know I love you," the little girl said. "Well, then, give me your pearls." "Oh! Daddy, not my pearls!" Jenny said. "But you can have Rosie, my favorite doll. Remember her? You gave her to me last year for my birthday. And you can have her tea party outfit, too. Okay?" "Oh no, darling, that's okay." Her father brushed her cheek with a kiss. "Good night, little one."

A week later, her father once again asked Jenny after her story, "Do you love me?" "Oh yes, Daddy, you know I love you." "Well, then, give me your pearls." "Oh, Daddy, not my pearls! But you can have *Ribbons*, my toy horse. Do you remember her? She's my favorite. Her hair is so soft, and you can play with it and braid it and everything. You can have Ribbons if you want her, Daddy," the little girl said to her father. "No, that's okay." her father said and brushed her cheek again with a kiss. "God bless you, little one. Sweet dreams."

Several days later, when Jenny's father came in to read her a story, Jenny was sitting on her bed and her lip was trembling. "Here, Daddy," she said, and held out her hand. She opened it and her beloved pearl necklace was inside. She let it slip into her father's hand. With one hand her father held the plastic pearls and with the other he pulled out of his pocket a blue velvet box. Inside of the box were real, genuine, beautiful pearls. He had had them all along. He was waiting for Jenny to give up the cheap stuff so he could give her the real thing.[43]

Waiting for <u>us</u> to give up the fake stuff; the cheap stuff; so He can take it, bless it and transform it, into the real thing.

---

43 *Internet Forward*

Eighteenth Sunday in Tempus per Annum (Cycle B)
(Exodus 16:2-4, 12-15; Ephesians 4:17, 20-24; John 6:24-35)

You must want to live.

It was once said: "Those who talk about the 'good ole days' didn't live then." I think some of that can be true. We talk about the past seeming to forget the difficulties we once had then, and glossing over the trials while looking at the present as the absolute worst possible situation. Reflection can yield much fruit in knowing where we came from. The miraculous of the miracle is in the fact that it happens subtly through nature. Miracles are all about timing. Think about it, if someone breaks a habit, or heals from an ailment after twenty-four years we think that is appropriate. Good things take time. However, if that same thing happened in a day, we call it a miracle.

God intervenes in our lives all the time, by removing the time it takes for something to occur (remember, a day is like a thousand years to God and a thousand years like a day.). The Israelites seem to be falling into a trap we often fall into ourselves. The trap of believing that it was not God who was responsible for saving us, but that we somehow saved ourselves. In the moment it happens, we can believe in miracles, until the dread of doubt comes in and shows us how much science can explain what happened, or how much we actually had to do with it.

Paul says it clearly: "Put on the new self, created in God's way in righteousness and holiness of truth." Many people can tell you the moment, time and date when they were saved. As Catholics, we say that we "are being saved" again and again. This is not something we can do ourselves, but something that God does for us. It is a gift, if we only accept it. The Israelites were willing to accept the gift when all seemed right in the world, but as soon as things became difficult; as soon as they were no longer seemingly "in control" they cursed the God that freed them. God grants them what they need and they will praise Him for the gift, and yet soon after they will again forget who it was; they will begin to have contempt for the gift that they so willingly received in the beginning.

> The inauthentic in us strives ceaselessly to resist and reject the life of Christ. In 1968, when Philip Blaiberg received a new heart during a surgical transplantation, and August of 1969, when he died, his entire body, from the brain to the least important cell fought with astounding ferocity and inventiveness to repel the new heart that, nevertheless was vital for him.[44]

We do the same thing. This inauthenticity within us which does not want to be ruled by a God, or a Church or religiosity or anything like Tradition is like the body that rejects the very Heart that is necessary for its survival.

Jesus says: "For the bread of God is that which comes down from heaven and gives life to the world." The word for life here "*Zoë*" is true, complete life. It is not the life called "*bios*" which is used to describe creatures, but the word to describe the heart, mind, soul, strength of us! This is the heart, which is restless until it rests in Him.[45] They were not looking for him because of the miracles. They were looking for him because he gave them something more than they ever had before. He created in them a longing. That for the first time in their lives, the body stopped fighting against the "heart" long enough that they felt that *life*…the real true life.

We have all been given the chance to be children of God. We have all been gifted with such a life to go out and make a difference in the world. And yet some of us have taken the bread, but not seen the signs. Some of us have been trying to save ourselves for so long, and we are no closer to becoming saints. Now is the time to make a change. Look around you in your life. You see people that are good and are faithful. I'm not talking about vain glory, or those who do it for appearances.

I mean the really faithful ones... the ones we wish we could be like because they are so good. What is it that they have? And what would it be like if for a moment, we lived life like them? Realizing that we really have no control over our salvation. I imagine it would be like a person holding their breath finally breaking through the top of the water that they thought was still miles above them. That is *life*. My God what a life! and it is yours. But you must want to live.

---

44 Fr. Peter G. van Breeman, SJ, Called by Name, (Denville, NJ: Dimension Books, 1976), 50.
45 Augustine: Confessions

Nineteenth Sunday in Tempus per Annum (Cycle B)
(1 Kings 19:4-8; Ephesians 4:30-5:2; John 6:41-51)

"There will come a time when you believe everything is finished..."

The Jewish authorities complained saying that Jesus was a *nothing*! The son of a carpenter. How is it possible that this kid (he was about my age) could know so much? How is it possible that such *riff raff* could become someone so influential? Isn't it amazing how sometimes we can be blinded by our own insecurities or flaws that we project our own helplessness on others? Isn't it amazing how we wish sometimes that we could change, but have no faith that change is possible in others?

The fact is, there was a time that I could relate with Elijah. "Elijah went a days journey into the desert, until he came to a broom tree, and sat beneath it. He prayed for death." I know you probably can't imagine that I would ever have a similar prayer, just as those authorities couldn't believe this humble carpenter's son could ever be anything more. But it's true.

I decided while I was in high school, that the possibility existed that I might possibly be a priest (I know, what were the chances, right?). Therefore, I was not going to involve myself with the drug scene or alcohol and all the things that go with the parties in high school and college. I stuck to this and was very devoted to the possibility that this might happen. The problem with such a pledge is that one might fall into something far worse than any of those things I was avoiding. And that is exactly what happened to me.

You see, when you take all of these things out of your life, and don't associate with people who do such things, you set yourself up as the judge and arbiter. You become the judge of everyone who does these things, and that is what I did. It wasn't enough that I isolated myself from these people, but I condemned them and reduced them to the worst thing they did. "We should never forget that every person is larger than his or her failings...If what we see in the other is only his or her failings, then we have ceased relating with the other in a fair way."[46] And because of this, I became an island unto myself, and I was miserable.

I remember such depression as I never felt before, and pray I never feel again. And as Elijah, I too prayed for death. Oh, I still prayed... but for death. And then one night, I will never forget, I was again praying for death. It was about midnight and the phone rang. It was a friend of mine across campus and she was ill and wanted me to walk her to the health center. Now the center was across campus in the other direction, but begrudgingly I did (I mean, she was one of my only friends at that point.)

We arrived at the center and I waited in the room outside of the offices. Finding myself with nothing to do but wait, I picked up a Reader's Digest and opened to "Quotable Quotes." There was a quote from a Louis L'Amore novel at the bottom of the page. I read the quote and for a moment it was like time stopped. And everything changed in that moment. I looked around to make sure I was alone and tore the page from the book. And up to a year ago, I still had the page, framed in my office. I recently lent it out to someone who needed it more than I.

> There will come a time when you believe everything is finished. That will be the beginning.
> —Louis L'Amour, *Lonely on the Mountain* (Bantam)
> 179

From that moment, my life changed forever. I made the decision that never again would I judge anyone, but would try to see the best in them. Paul's words to the Ephesians were an exhortation to do what

I found myself unable to do on my own. It would take a miracle for me to relinquish the "bitterness, passion and anger; the malice of every kind." That night I became an "imitator of God" who sees the best in us.

Is it possible that someone seemingly so far away from what God wanted him to be, could see the light in the darkness and become the one who is the face of God to people everywhere? You better believe it; because I do. What it requires is an openness to the Spirit. That on a late night on a campus in a most unlikely situation, an author that I never read before, and haven't read since would speak in a way that no one else could at that moment. Words that would give me hope in the midst of hopelessness allow me to see in myself the possibility I didn't see in others. The quote that read: "There will come a time when you believe everything is finished...that will be the beginning."[47]

---

46 Fr. Peter G. van Breeman, SJ, *The God Who Won't Let Go*, (Notre Dame, IN: Ave Maria Press, 1998), 124.
47 Louis L'Amore, *Lonely on the Mountain*, (Bantam Books, 1984).

Feast of the Assumption of the Blessed Virgin Mary
(Cycle B)
(Revelation 11:19a; 12:1-6a; 1 Corinthians 15:20-27; Luke 1: 39-56)

Mary's first Presumption...

Mary's first *Presumption*, led to her ultimate *Assumption*. And her first presumption was this: That whatever God asked of her, would be the absolute best for her. And *that* is why we celebrate her today.

TWENTIETH SUNDAY IN TEMPUS PER ANNUM (CYCLE B)
(PROVERBS 9: 1-6; EPHESIANS 5: 15-20; JOHN 6: 51-58)

How do you celebrate the Eucharist?

There was a person who went to someone's home for dinner. They arrived a bit late, but nonetheless the host was happy to see them. When they arrived they sat quietly, as though they were waiting for the main event to occur. The Host spoke with them and they answered with the least effort possible, as they adjusted themselves in their chair to find the most comfortable posture. This continued for about an hour, at which time dinner was served. The Host took special pleasure in offering a blessing, but the guest did not take part. They simply sat there in anticipation of the feast.

When the food was served, they greedily consumed what was placed before them, not savoring the flavor, or offering conversation. Once they finished the meal, they hastily got up from the table, put on their coat and walked out the door; there was no thanks offered to the Host, no goodbye, or *fare ye well;* simply a quick exit as though this meal was a small part of an extensive schedule for the rest of the day.

Now I ask you: How do **you** celebrate the Eucharistic meal?

Twenty-First Sunday in Tempus per Annum (Cycle B)
(Joshua 24: 1-2, 15-17, 18; Ephesians 5: 21-32; John 6: 60 – 69)

"Will you also leave?"

"Many of Jesus disciples listening said: 'this is a difficult saying; who can accept it?'" And Jesus said to the twelve: "Will you also leave?" What is so difficult? If we trace back to the previous week, Jesus says: "Whoever eats my flesh and drinks my blood has life within them" (*John 6: 54*). We cannot begin to understand what this means as Catholic Christians unless we understand our roots in Judaism.

In ancient Judaism, there was something called the "sin offering." This was an offering made to repair the relationship with God that was broken with sin. It required the sinner to bring to the priest an unblemished lamb. The lamb was slaughtered and its blood poured out on the ground, because the Jews believed that the *Nephesh* or life-force of God was in the blood. The priests would then eat the flesh and then offer some of the flesh to the people. This was for the forgiveness of sins.

Now, picture this: Jesus approaches John the Baptizer in the desert who proclaims: "Behold the lamb of God who takes away the sins of the world." Jesus is that lamb…led silently to the slaughter. An unblemished lamb. He is the sin offering, but not just any offering. This is the lamb "of God." The perfect offering who "takes away the sins of the world." None of his bones were broken but instead they lanced his side and blood flowed out followed by water. The blood was not spilled on the ground as with the lamb, however, but was given to us to consume; the blood which holds the life-force of God. Therefore we take the life-force of God within us…the presence of God within us or…GRACE! Why is this saying difficult?

"Part of the conviction that we are earthen vessels created by God the potter is the joy of finding we bear his fingerprints on our bodies and his breath in our Spirit."[48] The saying is difficult because if we are empty and open to the true presence of God, we will be changed. As Fulton Sheen once commented: "How can we expect God to transform us if we bring nothing to be transformed." "Do you also want to leave?" I believe Peter probably thought, "Yes, we do want to leave...but where?" We know the truth. And to know the truth and see where it leads... not to follow is impoverishment.

Are we empty vessels....are we prepared to receive the presence of God within us? If Jesus said today, "I wish to stay at your house today." How would we prepare? I don't know about you, but I'd probably leave right now and go clean my house. On second thought, I'd probably go rent a house for a day, because I would want it to be as perfect as possible! How clean is our house? Are we ready for the Lord, have we emptied ourselves, or are we full?

Joshua poses the question, "Who will serve?" People do not have to believe what we say, but they will believe what we do. Today we approach the altar of the Lord. The sin offering has been made, but are we ready to receive the Lord into our house. Are we prepared for the Divine to dwell in our home? Is this saying difficult? Will you also leave? Where shall we go, Lord? You have the words of everlasting life.

---

48 Fr. Warren Murrimen, OSB, Given in a homily at St. Gregory Chapel, St. Vincent Seminary, 2003.

Twenty-Second Sunday in Tempus per Annum (Cycle B)
(Deuteronomy 4:1-2, 6-8; James 1: 17-18, 21-22, 27; Mark 7: 1-8, 14-15, 21-23)

What does it mean to be a disciple?

"This people pays me lip service but their heart is far from me. Empty is the reverence they do me because they teach as dogmas mere *human precepts*." Wait, you're kidding me. Jesus is saying that?! Human precepts is what he called all the reverent things we're supposed to do. He's talking about what we read in the first reading from Deuteronomy, isn't he? Moses told them, "Hear the statutes and decrees which I am teaching you to observe that you may live..." What can Christ possibly mean then?

Paul explains when he says: "He wills to bring us to birth with a word spoken in truth so that we may be a kind of firstfruits of his creatures." "By their fruit you will know them" (*Mt. 7:16*). So what does this boil down to? Our lips can offer prayers; say "I love you;" and our minds can know all of the commandments. But knowing *about* and *speaking* of these things is not what God desires of us. What He desires is what is within... what He placed within to be brought without. That is what it means to be a disciple.

While in the Seminary, we were often visited by certain dignitaries: cardinals, bishops, governors, etc. It was not uncommon to see them walking around being given tours of the grounds. Now as a seminarian, I had my day pretty much scheduled for me. I had to pray, study, go to class, go to prayer, meetings, dinner, meetings, activities, meetings, choir practice, etc. One such day I was milling around thinking about all the things I had to do and running around trying to get them all done.

I lived on the third floor, and on this day I decided to take the elevator. (Not that I'm lazy or anything, I just had to justify that we had an elevator by taking it now and then!) But please understand me....this elevator was slower than death! You pressed the button and waited seven hours until the doors closed. It was then another seven hours until it began to ascend. So I'm standing there waiting for the doors to close....and then it happened.

You know, it's probably happened to you as well. I heard voices closing in. Now I don't mind telling you this because I know you won't judge me....right?.....but anyway, I began to formulate a plan. If the person saw me before the doors closed then I would let them in. I would stop the doors because *THEY* could identify me. But....if the doors closed and they didn't see me, then I was *home free*! And so I waited, and finally the doors began to close, but the voices were getting closer and closer.

The doors started closing and then he turned the corner and saw my face....it was a cardinal, and he looked right at me! So in an effort to stop the door from closing I threw my leg forward and when I did... all I saw was my sandal flying through the air... and then the doors closed. I had just kicked one of the highest ranking officials of the Church..... and I was just a seminarian!

As I began my long trip to the third floor (and I can't recall a longer trip) my first thought was...... "Man, that sandal's gone!" But as I continued my ascent, I thought, "Now why did you do that? Why couldn't you have held the door another minute?" Not just because it was a Cardinal, but for anybody. And then I reflected further: "Why was I at the seminary? I'm not here to pray, although that's most necessary. I'm not here to study, although that is important. I'm not here for the meetings and practices and activities, although they all play a role. I'm here to become more like Christ. If I'm not becoming more like Christ, then I have failed miserably." That day, I had failed miserably. So I decided, I'm going to find that Cardinal and apologize. Not for kicking him (because I didn't try to do that) but for my lack of charity.

I eventually made it to my room and got ready for the afternoon. I was heading down to class (this time I used the stairs) and I was approaching the notorious elevator. As I got closer I noticed there was something set on the bench facing the elevator. As I got closer I realized it was my sandal. As I continued my approach I also noticed there was a post-it note attached to it at this point. I picked up the sandal and read the note scrawled on the piece of paper and it read: "Thank you for trying."

Here, this man didn't know me from Adam, and yet he thought the absolute best possible scenario. (He had no idea how I had planned to leave him there if he didn't see me.) He saw the very best. He gave me the absolute benefit of the doubt. That trip in the elevator gave me a glimpse into how I was living my life in a way unfit for the kingdom. I had experienced true sorrow for the sin, and firm purpose to change those things. And when we do make a change, it is then that God smiles and gently takes us by the hand, and leads us to where we need to be.

What God seeks in us is the *disciple*. The disciple is the one who realizes that when we do not act in charity...all else is for naught. Now, we're not perfect. But as long as we try...as long as we make an effort to use the pious practices and "statues and decrees" to grow closer to God in charity, then even when we fail, God smiles and gently responds: "Thank you for trying."

Twenty-Third Sunday in Tempus per Annum (Cycle B)
(Isaiah 35: 4-7; James 2: 1-5; Mark 7: 31-37)

Our education in the faith never ends.

Have you ever worked on something for several hours in order to put it together by your own merit; instead of taking five minutes to read the directions and do it right? No? ...Me either, but do you know there are people like that? For an entertainment center or a bike or an appliance that *might* be an option...but it is not an option for our spiritual life. Too much is riding on our relationship with God to chance wasting time on our own merit.

Do you remember, when you were instructed in the faith, the first time you heard the commandments? Song: "First I must honor God; second honor His name....third keep His day holy, this will be my aim....adultery (whatever that is)." I remember this vividly in second grade. Then learning the sacraments...think about it: that God in his goodness knew that as beings we come to know through our senses. So that he would give us these outward signs of an invisible reality. That every sacrament occurs outside of time and space and yet affects us here within time and space. That for each symbol we see, something invisible is occurring. That is what we believe. So it is from Baptism to Holy Orders. That we learned the difference between a Mortal and Venial Sin. We learned our prayers: Our Father, Hail Mary, and Glory be, Angel of God; every day we prayed the Morning Offering, and every afternoon the Act of Contrition. That we prayed a decade of the rosary every day during Advent and Lent; and we were taught why fasting was so important. We read a story from the Bible every day. We were taught that fish wasn't considered "meat" and so we were permitted to eat it. We knew the stations of the cross by heart, and the *beatitudes*.

We look at these things and we see some instructions for memorization on a test; but if that is all we see, we've missed the whole point. These are instructions for life. I am grateful for having been raised in this manner, because I have the instructions to keep me on track. If I don't know the ten commandments, how do I know if I'm obeying them? How can I live by the beatitudes if I don't know them? How can I pray as a community with the Church if I don't know the prayers of the Church? If you were not raised with these things, or if you are a newcomer to the Church, I would encourage you (if there's not a stronger word) to investigate them and learn them.

We have a program in the Church called the RCIA. This stands for the Rite of Christian Initiation for Adults. This class is for those who wish to become Catholic; for those who have fallen away from the faith and wish to return; for those who are Catholic and want to learn more about their faith; or those who were never taught the ways of the Church. This is a wonderful opportunity for anyone who never had the benefit of instruction. There are Bible Studies. There are adult education classes in the Diocese. We have programs at the Diocese for all sorts of information. These are the instructions---we need only obtain them. Why? Because our Salvation depends on our relationship with Christ and the way we come to know Christ is through His word, and the tradition he left us.

What does this require of you? Today in the Gospel Jesus cures a man who is deaf. What is interesting is that the man did not approach Jesus on his own behalf. The man had sight, he could have sought out Jesus himself, but he didn't. The man's friends are the ones who brought him to Jesus; and that is what Jesus asks us to do for our own. If you are well versed in the faith and feel confident in how you are living the Christian life, Jesus wants you to lead your friends to him. If you know someone who is considering joining the Church, *YOU* bring them to RCIA. Let the know there's no obligation (Jesus never chased anyone down), but opportunity. If you know a Catholic who would like instruction in the faith, bring them to RCIA. And be there with them. The greatest gift we have from Christ is the Church. The greatest gift we can offer another is the Church. Many who need to hear this message will not hear it today from me….you take it to them, and give them that gift that will continue to feed them the rest of their life…the gift of an opportunity to encounter our Lord in perhaps a way they thought impossible.

Twenty-Fourth Sunday in Tempus per Annum
(Cycle B)
(Isaiah 50: 4-9; James 2: 14-18; Mark 8: 27-35)

"Who do they say that I am?"

Jesus poses the question, and the answer finally is clear. Peter, the one who usually sticks his foot in his mouth soon after opening it, states very clearly that Jesus is the Son of God, the *Messiah*. Jesus then validates that Peter surely is not speaking of his own wisdom, but because of the wisdom of God. Peter, now on a high because finally he gave the right answer, will be put in his place again, by Jesus who refers to him as Satan. But Peter doesn't walk away, he is not done yet, and because of his perseverance, and the patience of the teacher, Peter will be our first Pope.

Wishing to encourage her young son's progress on the piano, a mother took her boy to a piano concert. After they were seated, the mother spotted an old friend in the audience and walked down the aisle to greet her. Seizing the opportunity to explore the wonders of the concert hall, the little boy rose and eventually explored his way through a door marked "NO ADMITTANCE". When the house lights dimmed and the concert was about to begin, the mother returned to her seat and discovered that the child was missing. Suddenly, the curtains parted and spotlights focused on the impressive Steinway on stage. In horror, the mother saw her little boy sitting at the keyboard, innocently picking out three notes: doe, ray, mi. As she stormed the stage to remove the youth, the great piano master made his entrance and quickly moved to the piano, waving off the mother. He quietly approached the boy and whispered in the boy's ear, "Don't stop playing."

Then leaning over, he reached down with his left hand and began to play chords to match the notes the boy was playing. Soon his right arm reached around to the other side of the child, and he added a running melody to the three notes. All of a sudden a rhapsody ensued. Together, the old master and the young novice transformed this chaotic assembly of sounds into a wonderful *rhapsody*. These notes having seemingly no relationship musically now, captivated the audience. That night, they heard a composition they had never heard before, and would never hear again. The audience was so mesmerized that they wouldn't recall what else the great master played.[49]

Isaiah says: "The Lord God opens my ear that I may hear and I have not rebelled, have not turned back." Peter listened to the voice of God, even when it hurt. Even when the words of Truth seemed to contradict his convictions, or the way *he* thought things should "play out." The people at the concert that night, never would have witnessed such a moment of inspiration if a teacher would not have been willing to humble himself; and if the child who was looking for something had not persevered and listened to the voice of the master.

---

49 *Internet Forward*

Twenty-Fifth Sunday in Tempus per Annum (Cycle B)
(Wisdom 2: 12, 17-20; James 3:16-4:3; Mark 9: 30 – 37)

The want in us, sometimes keeps us from what is needed.

I will never forget my first anniversary as a priest. The day was so life-changing for me that I actually celebrate that, as a separate anniversary. It was my first anniversary, and I had plans to celebrate it with my family. I was planning for a private Mass in the afternoon for them and then we would go out to dinner and celebrate. I received a call at the parish that afternoon. It was from the medical center. One of our teens had made an attempt on her life and was in the psychiatric ward of the hospital. They warned me that she didn't want to see anyone, but the family was requesting that I go in to see her.

I was a bit disappointed at the timing as I had so many plans for later that day, but I called my parents and told them that I had to change the plans and what I was doing. Needless to say I was a bit put-out, thinking that I had to go see someone who really didn't even want to see me. I drove to the Med. center and went up to the psychiatric ward. I signed in with the ward nurse and she said: "Father, she's not seeing anyone right now. She's not talking to anyone." I replied, "Listen. She's darn well gonna see me today, I don't care if I sit there for an hour in silence, she's gonna see me." So I went in, and there she was.

She looked up for a moment and rolled her eyes. She told me I could give her a blessing and just leave, but as I stated before, I was going to stay for at least an hour. If she wanted to go to her room, she could, but I wasn't going anywhere. We sat and sat, until finally I opened my breviary (the book with the prayers priests and members of the Church pray five times a day) to Friday Compline (night prayer).

The psalm for this prayer is psalm 88. Now most of the psalms end on a happy note, or at least with some hope…but psalm 88 is not one of those. It ends by saying: "You have taken away my friends…my only friend is darkness." Well, if you're not ready to take the gas pipe when you read this psalm, you're certainly ready by the time it's over. But I was drawn to it and so I began to recite it aloud.

As I prayed this psalm, I saw her begin to look up, but I continued, pretending not to notice. Finally as the psalm finished, she had tears rolling down her cheeks and she said: "That's…in there?!" She couldn't believe that in such a holy book, someone had felt so alone… so abandoned by God. And our conversation began. We ended up talking for quite some time about everything. I would go on to visit her many times after and eventually she would recover. I returned that night to the Church and the place was empty. It was about 8:30 p.m., and everyone was gone and the place was locked up. I went into the chapel, vested, and celebrated Mass for my first anniversary as a priest, alone. And I have never felt more like a priest in my life, than at that moment.

What does Wisdom say? "Let us see whether his words be true… for if the just one be the son of God, he will take care of him." James says: "What you desire you do not obtain…you do not obtain because you do not ask." The gift God gave me that day was one I did not ask for, and would never have asked for. I had in my mind what I wanted, and therefore would not have had what I needed. Jesus gets so upset with the Apostles because they argue among themselves about what they think *they want*, instead of asking for the one thing *they need*.

If anyone wishes to come after him, they must be a servant…the one who serves despite their own wants. Thank God I was pressed into service that day, because I received a wonderful gift on my first anniversary. The gift of being a priest…the gift of doing what I was supposed to do in the first place.

Twenty-Sixth Sunday in Tempus Per Annum (Cycle B)
(Numbers 11: 25-29; James 5: 1-6; Mark 9: 38-43, 45, 47-48)

In the name of the Father, and of the Son, and of the Holy Spirit...

At that time, John said to Jesus:

"Teacher, we saw someone driving out demons in your name, and we tried to prevent him because he does not follow us." "There is no one who performs a mighty deed in my name who can at the same time speak ill of me." Notice the change there. The apostle says: "They do not follow *US*." Jesus is saying: "They need not follow YOU, but *ME*." This is important. What seems to motivate John to say this is not that the person was an affront to the Master, but that this person was not giving up what they had; was not following them around; was not taking after their example. There is no one who performs a mighty deed *IN MY NAME*. Those are the words that are important.

That phrase *"In my name"* is used twenty-eight times in scripture. Seventeen of these instances occur in the New Testament. Jesus says:

Receives a little child in my name
Does a mighty deed in my name
Asks for something in my name
Father will send the Holy Spirit in my name
Many will come in my name
Where two or three are gathered in my name

So we begin to see here, a distinction between: Following **US** and Following **Christ**. To do something in the name of another is to do it for them. We can do many virtuous acts, but who are we doing them for? If we are doing them in the Name of Jesus, then Jesus is the focus...not us. We are to be the clear glass through which others see

Christ. The apostles are enjoying some of the glory that comes with being an apostle of Christ; since they did not share in the glory of *this person*, they condemn him.

Of the seven deadly sins, the sixth most deadly is Vain Glory. Doing those things so that others might see them. But it goes beyond that. At times, we want people to follow US and not Christ. I'm not speaking about a desire to evangelize non-Catholic Christians, or even non-Christians. I'm speaking about alienating other members of our Catholic community because they do not do things *as we do*. They do not pray *as we do*; receive the Eucharist *as we do*; participate *as we do*, etc. Some of what I have observed as a priest is mislearned lessons which have turned into devotionals run amuck!

We must be very careful that we do not fall into the trap of the Israelites in the desert, who condemn those who were not conventually brought into the line of judges. We must be careful not to condemn the strange exorcist because he does not appear to be a part of our group.

When we were little we were not taught: "If you place a scapular over your bedpost, if you die in your sleep you will go to heaven." We were taught, if you have a scapular over your bedpost and you die in your sleep, the Blessed Mother will pray for you to go to heaven. Some have received papers called the *Irresistible Novena*, or the prayer that will guarantee salvation. People are under the impression that if they wear a certain medal or have devotion to a particular saint, then they need not worry about hell, that they will be saved. Non-Christians (let-alone Catholics) are burying statues of St. Joseph in their yards to sell the house…upside down. Tell me how burying a statue (possibly a holy object) can sell a house? (It's okay to laugh right now, acknowledging the fact that you've done this…I won't judge…much.) Try asking the saint to intercede for you. People will say: "It works!" So does a horoscope. I would propose we would do more good for the faith of the Church if we put our trust in Christ, and use sacramentals as a way to lead us to him; not back to US.

Do you see the problem here? By misusing these sacramentals that the Church uses to increase our faith, we are essentially removing the power from God. "If I do this, then it will happen." We are looking toward an idol instead of looking to God. We would openly condemn any religion that does this; yet we would condemn our fellow Catholics who do not. God forbid they follow US. They would not be acting in the name of Jesus.

Twenty – Seventh Sunday in Tempus Per Annum (Cycle B)
(Genesis 2: 18-24; Hebrews 2: 9-11; Mark 10: 2-16)

What does it mean to receive?

Sally was driving home from one of her business trip in Northern Arizona when she saw an elderly Navajo woman walking on the side of the road. As the trip was a long and quiet one, she stopped the car and asked the Navajo woman if she would like a ride.

With a word or two of thanks, the woman got into the car. After resuming the journey and a bit of small talk, the Navajo woman noticed a brown bag on the seat next to Sally.

"What's in the bag?" asked the old woman. Sally looked down at the brown bag and said, "It's a bottle of wine. Got it for my husband." The Navajo woman was silent for a moment, and then speaking with the quiet wisdom of an elder said,
"Good trade."[50]

A KEY phrase in the words of Christ today is this: *Whoever does not receive the kingdom of God like a child will not enter it."* What does it mean to receive? Jesus is dealing with two key issues here. The first has to do with the marital union, the second a child. I would like to address each of these, and yet each has to do with that statement on receiving.

What does it mean to receive? Comes from two Latin words: *re*, and *capio*. *Re* means again, and *capio* means accept. Accept again? Jesus refers back to the story in Genesis, in which the problem was not so much that Adam and Eve pursued an evil. What they were after was *a good*, something very good in fact. The issue was that the good, was not to be taken, but received. There is a difference. Whenever we sin, we are typically after a good, but sometimes it is a good we have no right to possess at that time. When you were little, to eat a cookie was a good, but not before dinner.

To receive is to allow another to give to us. A love that receives never takes. Marriages begin to dissolve when one or both take; in the same respect, marriages are already damaged when the two refuse to receive: that includes being open to receiving life as well. When we take what we have no right to, or refuse the gifts that are offered us, we make ourselves greater than God. The original sin of the evil one. So then what does it mean to receive?

There was a group on safari in Africa. One of the leaders got up early one morning and decided to hunt some breakfast for the group. He had bagged two wild turkeys and was walking back to camp when he got the distinct feeling he was not alone. He felt as though he was being watched. He stopped suddenly and looked around, but there was no one. He began to think that he was probably just spooked a little and continued walking. Again he felt eyes upon him as though now he was the one being hunted. Suddenly he turned and there before him stood a naked native boy. He looked emaciated and just stood there looking at the man. Very slowly, he unbuckled his belt and let the two turkeys fall to the ground. He then walked about twenty yards away and waited. The boy approached the two turkeys, but did not touch them. The man motioned for him to take them, that they were his, but the boy remained motionless, simply looking at the birds with longing eyes. This was more food than he had probably seen in weeks. Finally the boy reached out his hands towards the turkeys, but would not touch them. Slowly the man approached the boy, and very carefully picked up the two turkeys and placed them in the hands of the boy. The boy grabbed the turkeys, and with a smile took off into the woods and disappeared. To receive. The boy was unwilling to take the food in front of him; he was willing to go on starving rather than to TAKE what wasn't his.[51]

That brings us to the second part. To receive the kingdom like a little child. How does a child receive a gift? Without question; without reservation; with joy. We often look for the *quid pro quo* not possibly believing anyone could give so freely. Because we doubt that authenticity, we refuse to receive; we will not be hurt; we will not be obligated. We refuse the gift. God always gives in *Absolute gratuity*.[52] The gift cannot be traced back to the fingers that gave it. If we could receive such a gift, then we would never have the need to take, because the gift we were offered would be the only one we need. Take care of your gift.

---

50 *Internet Forward*

51 *Adaptation of a Story from Fr. Ronald Rolheiser, OMI, Against the Infinite Horizon: The Finger of God in Our Everyday Lives, (New York: The Crossroad Publishing Company, 2001), 68.*

52 *For more on Absolute Gratuity, Read: Emmanuel Levinas, Otherwise than Being or Beyond Essence, trans. Alphonso Lingis (The Hague: Nijhoff, 1981), 157, 159*

TWENTY-EIGHTH SUNDAY IN TEMPUS PER ANNUM (CYCLE B)
(WISDOM 7: 7-11; HEBREWS 4: 12-14; MARK 10: 17-30)

The price of Eternal Life

"God's word is living and effective, sharper than any two-edged sword. Nothing is concealed from Him; all lies bare and exposed to the eyes of Him to whom we must render an account." That's from the Letter to the Hebrews. "Him to whom we must render an account." So often, however, it seems the one we are rendering our accounts to is the *Spirit of this World*. We live for *this* world; we work for *this* world; we do whatever it takes to advance in *this* world. For this is the world we live in...we believe in. And if this world *is*, all there is, then eat drink and be merry, for tomorrow we die.

What we're talking about here is not simply a modern reflection on society. It has been there from the very beginning. Here comes the rich young man. He has it all...looks, talent, *bling*...even theme music...he has it all and yet he too is pursuing Jesus. He is looking for "eternal life." Upon reflecting on this passage, two things come to mind. The first is the question, why is he looking for eternal life? Now that may seem painfully obvious, but is it? He asks what he can do to inherit eternal life. Jesus tells him, and then he walks away sad. But why? He asked the question...he got the answer... what more is there?

Perhaps we should answer the question, why he wanted eternal life. In the end, we find out he's a rich guy. Wouldn't a rich guy want to be eternally rich? Sure! Therein lies the reason he was searching for eternal life. Once he found out he had to give up being rich, and then would have eternal life...he no longer wanted it.

The second issue to address is something specific here. Jesus says to him: "Sell everything you own, give the money to the poor and come follow me." Now, there's a question. Why did the guy have to sell everything he owned? Why could he not have simply given away all his possessions? How many of you have ever encountered what is called (for lack of political correctness) an "Indian Giver." To give away the possessions would not be enough, because he could always reclaim them. But if he sold those possessions, that would be a contract. To take them back would be stealing and this man prided himself in never disobeying a single commandment. And by giving the money to the poor, there was no chance of ever getting cash back.

What this means for us is that Jesus requires a total commitment. No luke-warmness here. If we are seeking eternal life, life which this world cannot provide for us, we have to be willing to surrender the one thing that keeps us from it. There are two words that could be used. The first "bios" means *life*, like a flower is living or an insect is living. That is not the word used here. The word this young man uses is *zoë*. This means full rich divine and human life. This is the fullness of life. But isn't this a rich guy? Doesn't he have everything? I mean he's following the commandments and has everything....except the only thing that matters....True Full Life. Life which we cannot secure for ourselves. We can only secure it having had an encounter with Christ, and allowing that encounter with Christ to change us forever.

Twenty-Ninth Sunday in Tempus Per Annum (Cycle B)
(Isaiah 53: 10-11; Hebrews 4: 14-16; Mark 10: 35-45)

One who is sent to "hoi palloi."

The preacher took to the pulpit and began his homily: "One day, everyone in this Church is going to die." As he said this, a little old lady sitting to the right began to giggle and a smile crept across her face. Despite this distraction, the preacher repeated: "One day, everyone in this church is going to die." Again, the lady smiled and began to giggle to herself. Finally the preacher could take it no more and he said: "Mrs. Livingston, what are you laughing at? How can you be laughing when I'm sayin' "One day everyone in this church is going to die?" She looked up and replied: "Reverend...I don't belong to this church."[53] *This* is not the mentality of an apostle...*one who is sent.* That is why Jesus takes the opportunity today to teach what it *does* mean.

These two apostles are fighting over which high place they can have. If we translate what they are saying, the conversation would go like this: "Lord, forget about those other ten guys....forget about all these people...let's get together the three of us and rule." You notice Isaiah says: "He would take the sins of many on himself." The Letter to the Hebrews talks about the priest who is not unlike us, who must be one of us, so as to save the many. The Greeks called *the many, hoi palloi* .

To be an apostle necessitates being a missionary. This is what we called "Mission Sunday" the day we celebrate in a special way our particular call to evangelize the world. Jesus is saying, unless you are *one of the many*; unless you care about *the many*, you cannot be my disciple. The second part of his statement will reinforce this. "Are you willing to drink the cup that I drink? Be baptized with the baptism of which I am baptized?" They say... "We can." They don't say... "We *will.*" So what is it that we are called to do?

> Francis Joseph was emperor of Austria and king of Hungary from 1848 – 1916, one of the longest reigns in history. It was also one of the most progressive. He could be strict, but mostly he reigned with kindness. Early in his reign an epidemic of cholera overran Europe. Francis was advised to leave Vienna and take refuge in Salzburg until the plague was over. "Will there be room enough in Salzburg for all my children?" asked the emperor. "Certainly, your majesty" replied his counselors, "there is plenty of room for all the royal family." "Is there really room for all my children?" the monarch repeated as he pointed from his palace window to the crowds below. "Look at all those people. They are my children. Should their father forsake them in danger? No, my beloved Viennese have always shared my joys and my sorrows. I will not abandon them in their hour of trouble."[54]

Neither can we abandon the *hoi palloi*...the many....those in our families and abroad, who are waiting to see the face of Christ.

---

53 *Internet Forward.*

54 *Msgr. Arthur Tonne, 5-Minute Homilies on the Gospels of Cycles A, B, C, (Green Bay, Wisconsin: Alt Publishing Co., 1977), 109.*

Thirtieth Sunday in Tempus per Annum (Cycle B)
(Jeremiah 31: 7-9; Hebrews 5: 1-6; Mark 10: 46-52)

This one, *could be His.*

"The Lord has delivered His people the remnant of Israel." This remnant, was called the *Anowim*; the poor and lowly ones of God. Those who others trampled over the years; those who were seemingly always exiled; those who were little less than dead in the eyes of those around them. And yet, those who treated the *Anowim* in this way were those who claimed to be "religious" or "faithful ones."

Bartimaeus is one of these *Anowim*. A man was only as good as his work, or what he could do for the community in the Ancient World. So Bartimaeus was about as good as dead. He had probably asked everyone for help, but none of the "faithful" had enough time to lend a hand, or be inconvenienced for one who could not possibly ever pay them back. You can hear the crowd as they shout for him to "shut up" and not take away from their time with Jesus. But the one who could see through to our hearts, could hear the cry of one of His *lowly ones*.

My spiritual director in the seminary was assigned in Rome as he received his doctorate. While he was there, he had such zeal that he wanted to "save the world". (I still want to save the world.) So he decided for an apostolate, that he would work with Mother Teresa's sisters right in Rome. What they would do is take the blankets from the homeless people and give them fresh clean blankets. Their ministry consisted of washing blankets every day, and distributing them to men who many times were mentally ill. Those individuals would sometimes spit on them, curse at them, and shout angry slurs at them. He decided to work with them.

The washing took place right on the streets and the sisters used five gallon buckets of soapy water to clean the blankets and then would hang them up to dry. Justin would pick up the blankets by the corners so not to get anything on his hands. Keep in mind, these men were homeless, so the blankets became their kitchens, bathrooms, and bedrooms. You can imagine the filth. As Justin was gingerly dipping the blanket in the water, so not to get his hands in it, he turned to his left and saw a sister cleaning her blanket. She was scrubbing; both hands elbow deep in this putrid water, just washing away, with a big smile on her face humming a tune. Meanwhile Justin was trying to figure out how to get the whole blanket wet without touching it.

He paused a moment in his cleaning and asked the sister if he could get fresh water. She smiled and said: "Now father, you know that water for us is at a premium. Your water is still fresh enough to do a few more blankets." He looked at his water....now a putrid gray. He could see the waves of heat and odor disturbing the air over the bucket and was almost sick. He looked next to him again and saw this nun smiling, humming and washing away.

Justin was getting angry, and a bit resentful. He was thinking, *what's she so happy about. This is not for me. I need fresh water if I'm supposed to do this work.* He was becoming more and more angry each moment, and continued to look at this nun, with her smiling singing face as though she were enjoying this. Finally it came to the point where he though he would burst and he was ready to lean over and choke the life out of this nun, if for no other reason than to stop the humming.....and then just as he turned to her, she lifted her blanket from the water and looked at it intently...and then looked at Justin and said: "Just think.... This one might be His." His? Justin stopped and thought about all the times he had recalled in stories, Jesus coming to people enfleshed as the poor, the sick and the needy.

This sister, and all the sisters were cleaning these blankets for these homeless, thankless men. They were cleaning each one as best as they possibly could with the thought that "this one" might be His. They were not seeing the ugliness of those who are marginalized, or the odor that comes with having nothing. These sisters looked at the *Anowim* and saw the One who created them. In recalling this story, Justin would relay to us the miracle that happened to him that day. It was not a miracle unlike that of Bartimaeus. For he who wanted to save the world; but was blinded by a worldly view, received the gift of sight!

All Saints Day
(Cycle B, given at Catholic High School)
(Revelation 7:2-4, 9-14; 1 John 3:1-3; Matthew 5: 1-12a)
Not for the Faint of Heart...

Our faith is not for the faint of heart. *Wusses* need not apply. There are plenty of those who will call themselves "Catholic" or "Christian". They will go to Church, when convenient...they will pray when convenient...they will be activists and protest when convenient...but when uncomfortable they will drop their faith like a cigarette butt out a window. That's what I mean by a *wuss*. I'm not talking about a coward, because at least a coward knows what they fear and are afraid of something. I'm talking about someone who is apathetic...notice the root "pathetic." We need people who are ready to be martyrs and missionaries...the future belongs to these people; not to the faint of heart. But the world would have you think differently. "The reason the world does not know us is that it did not know him... Everyone who has this hope based on him makes himself pure, as he is pure."

What does it mean to be a martyr and a missionary? It means that we are committed and convicted in our faith. These days the trend is to dawn armbands, or those magnets on our cars. Some people have so many of those magnets you don't know what they stand for, but simply that they support the magnet industry! The fact is, with a magnet a march or even a wristband, there is no commitment. We can take it off or put it on like an accessory. A commitment to something or someone is not an *accessory* to life...it *is* a life. The future is not for the faint of heart...it is for those who are committed. It's not enough to be committed however....what are we committing to?

"These are the ones who have survived the time of great distress; they have washed their robes and made them white in the Blood of the Lamb." Committing ourselves to something means really believing in it...understanding it...seeing the good in it. But how many things do we defend to the death that are not worth the time? I said those who are frail will protest when convenient...what does that mean? We protest uniforms; we are here...this is what you wear...we all wear the same...just do it? Will you complain when you are in corporate America and they have a dress code? Come on. Instead of protesting uniforms, why not protest those who cannot dress modestly.

We protest breathalyzer tests or drug and alcohol policies; why not protest those who make the tests necessary? Why not protest the scum that sells drugs to your siblings...your friends...even if that scum *might be* your siblings or friends? Why protest the music that is not played or the videos not shown: why not instead protest those who continue to use women as objects or view men as these animals. Why protest teachers and administrators who have an investment in you...when you should protest those who continue to teach you a lie that you don't need to be committed to anything, and that YOU deserve everything.

It's time to wake up! To start committing ourselves to the *One* who does have power over our very soul. These individuals who are uncommitted all have one thing in common...they listen to the voice of the world which is empty and yet they follow their precept that: "You can have it all....both, and." Be the one to stand for something in your life. Don't go with the crowd like so many fish in a school simply to be comfortable. But those things that you commit to...commit to something that is for the betterment of the world and yourself...not something that allows for a life of convenience.

Blessed are they who are persecuted for the sake of righteousness, for theirs is the Kingdom of heaven. Blessed are you when they insult you and persecute you and utter every kind of evil against you falsely because of me. Rejoice and be glad, for your reward will be great in heaven." There is no future for the faint of heart....no room for a *wuss* in the kingdom. The kingdom is for those who are *committed*. Who will endure bravely whatever persecution they face because they are not the mindless subjects of this world. These are the ones who are "set apart" and that is why they are called holy....*sanctus*...that is why they are called *Saints*.

Thirty-First Sunday in Tempus Per Annum (Cycle B)
(Deuteronomy 6: 2-6; Hebrews 7:23-28; Mark 12: 28-34)

We cannot possibly love God if we do not love what He created good.

Take a few moments and make a list in your head. List all the things you hate about yourself...go on...take a few seconds. Now, take a few seconds to list all the things you love about yourself...that's right, I said *love*. Things you can do, characteristics you have, all the good things about yourself. Unfortunately, I would dare to make a wager that when you were asked to write the things you hate about yourself, most of you could begin immediately, and would only have stopped if someone stopped you. When I asked you to list the things you love.... there was a pregnant pause...and only then, you might have jotted down two or three. For *most* of you.....Why?

Perhaps it's from a lack of confidence, an insecurity; perhaps it's from a skewed perception of what pride and humility are; perhaps it's what we were brought up to think. I remember bringing one of my girlfriends by my Uncle Ickey once, and he said to her: "You're prettier than a daisy in spring." As only he could say it. She blushed and said, "Aw, that's nice" and something to the sound of "I'm not that pretty." And he abruptly stopped her (which was a surprise, because he did nothing abrupt) and he said: "Now look honey. There's nothing wrong with being pretty. You don't have to be humble when people point out the obvious...you just have to say 'thank you.'"

He made a great point. Thank you, isn't a response necessarily to my uncle (although she said it after that short lecture). *Thank you* should be mouthed as we look to the heavens. Whenever we receive a compliment we say thank you (Lord). So why can we not list the things we love about ourselves? Perhaps because we've neglected loving ourselves for so long, we've forgotten who we *are*. Listen to what Jesus says to the scribe, a new commandment: "The first is this: 'Hear, O Israel! The Lord our God is Lord alone! You shall love the Lord your God with all your heart, with all your soul, with all your mind, and with all your strength.' The second is this: 'You shall love your neighbor as yourself.'"

Love God with everything we have, and love our neighbor as ourself. Easy, huh? But I would propose this…we cannot love God, if we do not love our neighbor, and we cannot possibly love our neighbor if we do not love our self! This is not a narcissistic love, but a recognition of the fact that we are the very best God could make. This does not mean we are satisfied with ourselves either, if we are severely underweight or overweight; addicted to something; lazy; greedy; etc. It means we are happy with what God gave us as our life at this moment, and we see the best, while continuing to allow the Lord to move us beyond our own expectations.

Think about it. Before you were a father or a mother, a sister, uncle, CEO, lawyer, etc. who were you? Before you were a student; babysitter, employee, who were you? Sometimes we can become so consumed by the function or definition placed upon us, that we can lose the person we are. Sometimes we are so focused on the things we must do for others, that we lose our identity in the mix. I am not saying that family is not important, but that originally God created us as an individual towards a purpose and relationship with Him. Where is that journey right now? How have we progressed? Or are we so consumed with what we "*DO*" that we've forgotten who we were meant to *be*?

One of the greatest walls we face in our Love of God is that we cannot love ourselves. We cannot remember the time before we were defined by what we do. Think about yourself, as your *SELF*, in the solitude which is your condition as your SELF and love the person you are because it is the best God could create. If you can do that…then you are ready to love your neighbor. First Moses says to the Israelites: "Fear the Lord" because they did not know a God who was there. Then they are to Love Him. Only when they realize they are God's beloved and can love themselves, can they begin to love others.

So we begin with what the world would say "It's all about YOU." We begin at the end of the commandment with YOURSELF and work towards God. So Love yourself, then you can love your neighbor. And if you can love a human with a complete love, then you are ready to love the Divine.

Benedict XVI says this in *Deus Caritas Est*: "The unbreakable bond between love of God and love of neighbor is emphasized. One is so closely connected to the other that to say that we love God becomes a lie if we are closed to our neighbor or hate him all together."[55] Therefore, when we love ourselves, despite our shortcomings, we are able to love our neighbor. So next week I will talk about the way in which we can truly love our neighbor. For your personal prayer and reflection this week, however, look at the person deep within; the one that God created and love *THAT* person. And then all the things that have crept in over the years which are NOT of the person God created…those things which we hate (not ourself) offer to the proposition that "Any one, can…at any moment…begin a new future."

---

55 Pope Benedict XVI, Deus Caritas Est. Encyclical Letter, (Vatican City: Libreria Editrice Vaticana, 2006), §18.

THIRTY-SECOND SUNDAY IN TEMPUS PER ANNUM (CYCLE B)
(1 KINGS 17: 10-16; HEBREWS 9: 24-28; MARK 12: 38-44)

God sends us challenges when we need to grow in love.

Benedict XVI says this in *Deus Caritas Est*: "The unbreakable bond between love of God and love of neighbor is emphasized. One is so closely connected to the other that to say that we love God becomes a lie if we are closed to our neighbor or hate him all together."[56] But we cannot love our neighbor unless we first love our "self". Don't mistake this for a narcissistic love. It is very true that these days we have been called one of the most self-centered *generation* in the world…but that is not loving the *self*….that is "*being in love* with the *self.*" There is a difference. Ego-centrism is not love; it is insecurity. Think about how often people, in order to make a change in life will change their hair or nails; change their car or lose weight; go out and buy something to "make life better." But in all these things we are unwilling to change our "self." I would propose that the first step to changing our neighbor might just be to change our **self**.

Why can't we love our neighbor? Think about all the reasons why this is impossible. They are selfish; annoying; needy; a pain; irresponsible; crass; dirty; etc. etc. etc. We can come up with a list longer for some neighbors than we could when looking at our own bad traits. It's true…people are tough to love at times. There is no sacrifice in loving someone who is truly lovable. We love a puppy, until it stains our new carpet. Bad habits; traits; and idiosyncrasies do a lot toward helping us not to extend love to our neighbors.

Take a moment and think about one of those neighbors who is tough to love. Think about all of their characteristics; bad habits; perhaps things they do to offend you every chance they get. Got all that? Now imagine something for a moment. What would it be like if something happened tonight…they go to bed tonight and a miracle occurs, so that when they wake up tomorrow, they will no longer have those annoying traits. How would their life be different? How would you treat them differently? How would your life change?

The reason I bring this up, is that there are certain things in life which are well within our control. There are others, which are not. The fact is those people we do not like, are not within our control to change. WE cannot change them. The only one we can control is our "self." But yet, we are called to love them. So we are stuck, right? I don't know. Since we can't control them, we can only control ourselves. What if WE decided to change. What if I went to bed tonight, and imagined that a miracle occurred to that person and changed them. What if I got up tomorrow and treated that person as though they experienced a transformation, a miracle (even if they did not)? They would have to react.[57] So how would our attitude change? We would act as though we liked them, and would overlook some of the things that we dislike. It is not being fake; it is extending the gift of possibility to someone who perhaps hasn't had it before. CS Lewis says: "When you are behaving as if you loved someone, you will presently come to love him."[58]

The Gospel and first reading speak of this today. The widow who offers all she has, is doing the right thing. The Pharisees are not. However, I cannot imagine that some of those who witnessed the faith and devotion of this woman were not forced to change their ways. The widow of Zarepeth who was gathering twigs, was willing to accept the prophet as he was, and do as he asked as was dictated by hospitality, and he rewarded her for a lifetime.

The fact is, we cannot change other people, but sometimes, if we take the first step, and act as though they are already the person we would react to positively, we will be amazed at the vast change that can occur….look for such a change. We cannot do this unless we first love our "self." Someone who is insecure has no hope of ever extending such a possibility to another.

The Pharisee who has long robes was not respected because of his robes. He was the only one impressed by his clothes. He was in love with himself, but because of that, was unable to extend love to the Widow. The ones who were changed by this Widow (and obviously someone was because we're reading about it 2000 years later) were able to love their neighbor as they were called to do. When we can find God in our neighbor then, despite their brokeness, we are well on our way to Loving God with our whole heart, soul, mind and strength. And so next week, I will close with the way we can keep the highest commandment. If we love our self, then we have the capacity to love our neighbor, which naturally will lead to a love of God. As Benedict XVI states in *Deus Caritas Est*: " 'Worship' itself, Eucharistic communion, includes the reality both of being loved and of loving others in return. A Eucharistic which does not pass over into the concrete practice of love is intrinsically fragmented."[59]

---

56 *Ibid., §18.*

57 *Based on Theories of Charles Allen Kollar, Solution-Focused Pastoral Counseling: An Effective Short-Term Approach for Getting People Back on Track, (Grand Rapids, Michigan: Zondervan, 1997), 67-94.*

58 *C.S. Lewis, Mere Christianity, (San Francisco, CA: Harper Collins Publishers, 1980), 131.*

59 *Pope Benedict XVI. Deus Caritas Est. Encyclical Letter. (Vatican City: Libreria Editrice Vaticana, 2006). §14.*

THIRTY-THIRD SUNDAY IN TEMPUS PER ANNUM (CYCLE B)
(DANIEL 12: 1-3; HEBREWS 10: 11-14, 18; MARK 13: 24-32)

Without expectation…

Benedict XVI says this in *Deus Caritas Est*: "The unbreakable bond between love of God and love of neighbor is emphasized. One is so closely connected to the other that to say that we love God becomes a lie if we are closed to our neighbor or hate him all together."[60] But we cannot love our neighbor unless we first love our "self".

How do we know when we love God more than all else…? We are ready to *go*. This world often views death as the ultimate failure. Death is only a failure if nothing is to follow. But…if death is the only way to obtain the ultimate adventure…then we should not so much fear death, as embrace it. If we love our 'self' we will have a peace; a peace which allows us to truly love our neighbor. And if we love our neighbor as we should, we can begin to see the face of God in all we meet. If we can do that… successfully, then we have a foretaste of what is to come, and there will be no fear…only longing.

So how do we love God? With no expectations. The same way we must love our neighbor. True love is a gift of self to another. To give, is to give without conditions, without agendas, without expectation of return. When we give in this way, we will never be disappointed. The end times are not a threat to one who loves in that way. Now don't get me wrong, we *are* supposed to have expectations of people for high morals; to try hard at academics and sports, etc. Those are expectations that benefit them. I'm talking about a love without expectations that will benefit ME. Love without expectation means I love them simply for their own sake. That if we believe love is *self gift*, then this is giving a gift without any strings attached.

Do you know how freeing that IS? When we can love without expectation we do not need to promote ourselves, we are not insecure, we do not allow the moods of others to determine what ours will be.[61] Think of the people in your life now. Some of those we meet in the hall or out in the lot, and they are the people who always need something from us. And we think: "Oh man, what do they need now...what do they want now?" and we avoid them. What about those people who will do anything for us, or give us anything and never ask for return? They are magnets! Because we can see in them a glimmer of God. That is what we are called to be!

> CS Lewis says, however:
> "To love at all is to be vulnerable. Love anything, and your heart will certainly be wrung and possibly broken. If you want to make sure of keeping it intact...wrap it carefully round with hobbies and little luxuries; avoid all entanglements. Lock it up safe in the casket or coffin of our selfishness. But in that casket---safe and dark, motionless airless---it will change. It will not be broken; it will become unbreakable, impenetrable, irredeemable. The only place outside of heaven where you can be perfectly safe from all the dangers and perturbations of love is hell."[62]

I would like to close with a song. Warning: I am not a singer, so just bear with me as I return to God the voice He gave to me. I believe this is the dialogue between many of us, and God as we seek to love Him as we are called to do.

Group Name: Saving Jane   Song: *You Say*

> I've been calling and calling for you
> But you answer and I shut my mouth
> I've been searching and for you, but myself I don't want to be found.
>
> You say I am
> You say let go
> You say believe

But it's not that easy for me
You say wait
You say right now
Don't you see your already one foot at the ground, You say

I've been wicked and wild and wrong and I've wondered the price of
my shame.
I've been hiding my face for so long it's a wonder that you know my
name.

You say come home
You say I'm here
You say there's some things you just can't control.
You say let me
You say believe
Why do you search for the answers you already know?   You say

I am the way
and the light and the truth
Don't be mislead by the flight of your youth.
Have faith in the things you can't see to believe.
what if you had faith in me?

You say rest here
This is your home.
Don't you see that you knew I was here all along? You say[63]

---

60 *Pope Benedict XVI. Deus Caritas Est. Encyclical Letter. (Vatican City: Libreria Editrice Vaticana, 2006).*
 §18.

61 *Based on Readings from: Fr. Anthony DeMello, SJ, The Way to Love: The Last Meditations of Anthony De
 Mello, (New York: Doubleday Press, 1991).*

62 *C.S. Lewis, The Four Loves, (New York: Harcourt, Brace and Company, 1960), 169.*

63 *Saving Jane. "You Say" from Girl Next Door, (Umvd, Labels, 2006).*

CHRISTUS REX
THIRTY-FOURTH SUNDAY IN
TEMPUS PER ANNUM
(CYCLE B)
(DANIEL 7: 13-14; REVELATION 1: 5-8;
JOHN 18: 33-37)

What effect has the Jesus Event had on us?

The readings for the last few weeks have centered on the end of life. Both the end of our particular life (when we die) and end of universal life as we know it. We might be tempted to see this as some kind of failure. Much of society seems to see death through this lens, which is witnessed by the countless billions spent on preserving ourselves every year. But as Christians, we look at this end as the end to a world that was never meant to last. We look at death as the only way to obtain what was meant for us from the beginning. Because of the *Jesus Event*, his death for us, we have been saved from this world to live in the next; but how has this event impacted our lives? Do we really believe it? Or is it simply a story from the distant past, with no effect on our future.

I was up at my hermitage last week in the mountains, where I go to pray and for quiet. But when I'm up there, I'll usually go out one day for breakfast at a local diner, "Sherman's Valley Diner." I walked in last week, and the owners and workers know to look for me about once a month or so. They're friendly and down to earth. I listened to a dialogue between a fifty-five year old woman and an eighty year old man. Both had had some kind of heart surgery. The fifty-five year old woman, strangely enough, had a four bypass surgery, while the man had a valve replacement. Both were very animated in talking about their second lease on life. The old man said that if it had been a few years ago, they would not have been able to save them. The woman, with a similar story, had a heart attack, and they brought her back. Both were attributing this to a miracle, and they realized that they should not be there right now, but were given a second chance. And as I continued to observe the two, the woman picked up a bite of the sausage gravy over biscuit that she was eating, while the old man held a donut in one hand and a slab of bacon in the other.

Each had been given a new chance at life, and yet they were living as if nothing had happened. Are we doing the same? Do we realize the great gift we have in the redemption of Christ. Are we trying to become new people, or have we simply resigned ourselves that "this world *is* all there is"? In the dialogue between Pilate and Jesus we see a remarkable change. Pilate questions time and again in a cynical vein, this non-threatening man Jesus. He says: "Are you the king of the Jews." Jesus never really answers the question, but puts it in Pilate's mouth. "You have said it." What is remarkable is that as Jesus is crucified, Pilate will insist, to the chagrin of the Jewish authorities, that a sign be placed above the head of Jesus which reads*: This is Jesus of Nazareth, King of the Jews.* Jesus was right, "You have said it." The Jesus event had an impact even on the life of a Pagan…even on the life of a pagan Leader. What kind of effect has it had on you?

REFLECTIONS
APPENDIX I
RETREAT AT THE CAPE
OUT OF THE WOODS

I am on retreat. It worked out nicely because I have a wedding at the end of the week. The retreat was needed, but the wedding came first in the plan. The wedding was going to be on Cape Cod and therefore, I had to find a place on the cape. Conveniently enough there was a place and so it worked out. The first day of retreat was wonderful. I got up late (around 7am) and got changed, showered, etc. I celebrated Mass at 8am and then had a simple breakfast. Until noon, I read and reflected and wrote. I reflected that morning on the original rebellion of the angels, and on the passion of Christ. After lunch I decided to take a walk out on the cape. These priests own 180 acres of land, so I figured no place was off-limits. I began my walk out towards their inlet beach where the boathouse was. But I continued to walk. I prayed the rosary all the while and continued to walk.

I came to a spot where there was no more beach, just grasses mixed with swamp and rocks, but I continued to walk. I walked out into the water a bit. Whenever I got close to the grasses, these birds which looked like sandpipers would start shrieking at me. Then all at once, they began to dive at me. I have never been attacked by a bird before in my life and here they were. Had they known they were attacking a guy who had their relatives on wooden pedestals in museums, they might have thought different. These New England rebel birds. Just as soon as I would clear one patch of grass, another flock would start. But I continued to walk around this cape and soon more beach appeared and the birds left me alone.

I had walked for about two hours and wanted to get back up to the road. I presumed that where I saw houses in the distance that there would be a road. I continued around the cape and towards those houses, all the while thumbing my beads. Now near the beach, there was this platform about thirty feet off the ground and at the top a huge nest. If you thought the little birds were bad this large nest belonged to two Opreys. They began to cry out and the two mates took off from the nest and dove for me. Now little birds are one thing, but talons.... that's entirely different. Ever wonder why falconers wear those thick leather gloves? But that wasn't all; two more came from the distance towards me as well. I was running with these *crocs* on (that's right...my beach rubber sandals) away from the nest while trying to keep my eyes on them as well. (Go ahead..take a minute and visualize this; I'll wait) Do you think Jesus ever ran into this problem on the Sea of Galilee? It was crazy, they were actually trying to take me down. Finally I was clear of the nesting pair and they returned to their roost, while the other two escorted me to international air space.

So much for my spiritual walk, I just wanted to get back to the retreat house. I finished praying the rosary (fifteen decades by this point) and then next to one of the houses I saw a truck pull up. Finally, a road leading out of here. I walked to the houses, but by the time I got there, the truck had pulled away. I saw no road coming from these two houses anywhere. Was it a mirage? I had no clue. There was only a small path leading up through the yard to the left of the last house. I was tired, hot, and had to use the facilities so I decided to take the chance. I walked up through the yard and it was a log yard, with a mill, etc. It had a bunch of trucks, so I was just looking for the drive-way. Well, there was none. I mean, come on, there had to be a way in here. But I saw none, and there were people at the house, so I quickly made my way to another path I saw in the woods. I had to be getting closer to the road because I saw all the high trees were gone and there looked like a clearing. Also, there were telephone wires going along the trees, and I knew they would go along the road. Thank goodness. It was only about twenty yards between me and this clearing. I was prepared to go through anything to get there, if I could just get through. This was no problem. I had to pass through a little brush but that was it...Never AGAIN.

My first step, I sunk into moss and humus up to my knee, almost losing my shoe. The second step was much the same, a slurping suction sounding as I carefully removed my foot from this mouth of detritus.

It was like walking through…well, wet humus sludge. I could smell the bacterial gases as I removed my foot, a protest from the fauna whose sleep I had disturbed. So I began looking for patches of grass to stand on, and they were few and far between. There were these thick bushes, intermeshed with each other so that I couldn't go over and could barely go under. But I knew that on the other side of those bushes there was freedom from the heat, bugs, and threat of poison oak? Ivy? Sumac? (What do they have up here?). I figured the best way was simply to push through them like hedges. So I plowed through them, only to feel the recurved needles slice like a razor through my flesh. Mercifully, some of the thorns just cut through, while others made their home in my skin. These bushes had thorns!

As I pushed through they stripped the flesh from my bare legs and hands. Now I was in the midst of them and couldn't get out. The bushes were about 8ft high and just too thick. There was only one alternative. I dropped to my hands and knees, and as I did this, both hands plunged deep into the humus leaving my face only inches away. The scent singed my nostrils. I rolled in order to free my arms from the bog, turned on my belly and crawled under the tunnel made by their intertwining branches. The beetles and biting flies observing this spectacle followed like a group watching a golf tournament, wondering, is he gonna make it around this dog-leg, and then continuing on as I did. I sunk less in the humus because of my surface area, but I was covered with the muddy stinky bacteria-rich humus. My legs were leaving behind bloody moss as I dragged my knees and feet across some thorns hidden among the mosses. I just wanted to get out, and if that was the road, then it was worth it. I finally got to the telephone pole! Victory! I had overcome the forest, but then my countenance fell like the man who spends his last dollar on the race and his horse never leaves the stable…it wasn't the road. The telephone pole was surrounded by these thick thorny bushes, and there was no trail. There was a clearing of trees only because of these scrubby plants, through which nothing else could grow. But hope beyond hope, it looked like another clearing up ahead. I simply had to get through some more of these bushes.

The original twenty yards might as well have been twenty miles. I had planned later in the day to walk the stations of the cross these priests have in the woods; at this point, I felt as though I were *living* them. Once again, I dropped to my knees and crawled in the underbrush, now cutting my neck and hands again. I no longer noticed my legs burning, perhaps it was the humus-mud caked on like those beauty masks people wear. Because I was coated with the muddy humus though, it seemed the only blood the biting flies were getting came from the cuts on my legs or the trail I left in my stead. I made it to the clearing finally, and yet another disappointment... it wasn't a clearing at all. Just an area around a rotted tree. I climbed the tree and looked around. I saw no road...no way out. It was hopeless. I noticed the small dots now climbing up my feet; deer ticks like little seeds of a fresh kiwi orienteering in the part of flesh still not covered with mud. I was hot and tired and trapped.

I knew that if I followed the telephone lines surely they would eventually get to the road. I was in the woods and lost; that was my only hope. I was charging through these bushes and then would hit the thorns and just stop, frustrated that I couldn't move. I was getting desperate and felt trapped. I knelt down and prayed for guidance. Then I heard it... a bird was letting out squeals. It worked for St. Francis, why not for me. I thanked God for His mercy and goodness, and then followed the squeals. As I got closer to the telephone poles the squeals got louder and more frequent and I thought, this is amazing! This bird is leading me out. I was going through these plants knowing that I would not be back-tracking, and so doing what I needed to do in order to get to the sound. Finally more squeals; there must have been a dozen birds, all squealing frantically. I was almost there, and then I stopped...frozen. I realized what it was they were squealing about. The small bush in front of me...the one I was getting ready to push down, contained seven small nests. They weren't squealing for me at all! They were squealing because I was getting to close to their nests. All the birds on this cape had a conspiracy against me! I *was* a bird-lover too...until now.

I was done! Trapped again in these blasted thorns; bleeding from my arms and legs, I was spent. I turned to retrace my steps but there were no steps. I couldn't even see how I had gotten here in the first place. I was at my wits end. And I turned again to prayer. The name that came to mind was Jerry. This was a man I got to know just a few years before he died. He was an outdoorsy kind of guy and I knew he had a better view of the situation and so I asked. I finished my prayer and turned to go out but lost my balance because the moss had sucked in my foot and I fell hard; my hand and wrist plunging into the mud…right next to a very large paw print. Now, I don't know if they have bears up here, but if it wasn't a bear, it was a pretty big dog. That was my first thought. My second was the answer to my prayer: follow this critter's *path of least resistance.* That's what I did.

On hands and knees I followed his sunken pad prints through the underbrush. It was amazing that although the thorn bushes were still there, this creature had found the best path through which to pass. There were still thorns, and pain but not nearly as much. I pushed back the last bush and the breeze almost took my breath away as it enveloped me with coolness and the sun blinded my eyes. It was a clearing! Not simply a crowd of thorn bushes or a place where trees were not, but a true clearing with soil and rocks and ferns. There was no road or wires, but a clearing with none of those thorn brushes. I thanked God for leading me out and offered a prayer of thanksgiving. I scanned the surrounding area and saw a blaze orange ribbon around a tree. It was a hunter's mark. I went to it and looked around until I saw the other one, and then went to it. The last one was near the road. I stopped and thanked the Lord that I had found the road.

I immediately began running in the direction of the retreat house, only to my dismay to find that this road lead me to the beach I had walked along before entering the woods. This was the beach where the large birds had attacked. This was the road that I had seen the truck on, an hour before but because of the high dune I hadn't noticed it when I walked by. There were the telephone wires coming out of the woods. I immediately turned around and headed in the other direction. I was running with these crocs on; bleeding legs and arms and a muddy dirty face and body. I saw two women walking, (I must have been a site) and very casually asked where the main road was, as though I were just taking a walk. They said it was up ahead about a hundred yards.

I began to run, just yearning for civilization, when out of the corner of my eye, I saw a plank with a leaf-shaped plaque at the top; and at the top of the plaque, a cross. It looked like a station. The Stations of the Cross! I had found the retreat center. I ran through the woods to that station and it was the third station, Thank God! I was only at the beginning of the stations through the woods. Although I felt as though I had far surpassed the third station in my journey. I ran past the station and there was the cottage, just as I had left it. A four hour excursion and now back home, beaten, bloodied and tired. I was told later by the priests that the poison ivy in the woods is so thick that they won't walk there certain times of years. They went on to inform me of the problems they have with lyme disease and the biting flies. Looking back, isn't it amazing that the first thing I did, upon entering the woods was to cover my body with a muddy protective layer, much to my disgust; a muddy layer that preserved me from poison, flies, and other maladies. I pulled the ticks off as I left the woods, and to this point haven't had any side-effects.

My meditation that night was on the crucifixion. As I knelt in prayer for my 61 minutes I realized that the pain I felt that day; the cuts; solitude; lost; was only a faint shadow of the pain *he* realized during *his* life. And his physical pain, simply a shadow of the true agony caused by our willful separation from him.

Appendix II
First Meditation:
The first temptation; the first sin

The angels were created instantaneously. Imagine, full infused knowledge and wisdom of all things in the universe, in time and space and beyond. Beings of light, all in the presence of God. Can you imagine, infused knowledge? Perfect understanding of everything at one time. With all of that, we might fall into the temptation of believing it was us. That we were doing this by ourselves. I have no doubt that all of the angels were tempted. Think about it…how could one *not* be tempted? That all of them looked at the beauty which they were; they looked at all they were given and all they could do and if even only for a brief moment, they were tempted to believe that they were gods. And then they were told their creative purpose was to serve the creatures. The first temptation.

Free will cannot be harnessed. By its nature it is unshackled by everything but itself. And so a fundamental decision had to be made. Would they serve another with their free will; with all the gifts they were given…or would they serve self? Many, despite the temptation placed before them, chose to serve…others chose otherwise.

As soon as the decision was made, the change was instantaneous. Those who chose not to serve were separating themselves from God; separating themselves from pure Light, pure Beauty; pure Goodness. The change was instantaneous as their bodies were stripped of the light and the dark grotesque ugliness of the rebellious creature broke forth. The blackest cancer we can see is the fairest of their race. Because they were now without God, they were light-less; beauty-less; good-less. Every creature of this world, ugly as they might seem has some characteristic beauty, "because God who is beauty itself has fallen in love with them."[64] But not these creatures. So vast is the separation between them and God that the void casts a dark ugliness that steals life from anything it touches. These creatures, having been stripped of the light can no longer endure the light; it burns their bodies and yet

171

they are not diminished. It casts light on the ugly darkness which is their flesh and drives away the coldness of their wills, now frozen for eternity with their "I will not serve". Unable to *endure* the light, they flee to the farthest reaches of eternity where light no longer penetrates; the coldest depths of infinity so that the ugliness of their rebellion is hidden even from themselves. And there they remain in their eternal frustration; every moment in timeless eternity re-living the moment they chose their lot....all of them fled; except for one.

Yet even in this bitter grotesqueness one remains to curse God. This one who was once the bearer of light, can no longer stand the glow, and yet he ignores the cutting blades of light through his flesh as a final act of defiance. He is not satisfied with simply denying God, but seeks to destroy God. Even the mighty Seraphs were not immune to the temptation of Deity. He approaches the throne as an equal, and yet is dwarfed by the pure light of the Almighty. And in his defiance he smiles; no longer the luci-fer but the tempter and accuser. He would spend eternity drawing others into his dark ugliness by convincing the humans of their own ugliness. He would convince them of the absence of a God; convince them of their own godliness, and when he could not deliver the fulfillment they desired, he would accuse them of *his* very sin. He would try to convince them of the despair that he felt eternally. He smiled, because he saw in his knowledge the person of Christ; and His seeming failure on a hill in Jerusalem. Then as he looked around the realm of non-time and non-space he saw a vast number, too many to be counted; he a cherub was not intimidated by these less than he. But not wishing to lower himself to chill the light of their bodies, he thus departed until an opportune time. It was the sixth day.

---

64 *Fr. Peter van Breeman, SJ, The God Who Won't Let Go, (Notre Dame, IN: Ave Maria Press, 1991), 24..*

APPENDIX III
SECOND TEMPTATION: ADAM AND EVE

Sin is a crazy thing. Why would anyone commit a sin. Let's face it, would anyone want to separate themselves from true Beauty? True Goodness? True Light? Of course not. So why do we choose sin? Because it's delicious as one of my Theology professors used to say. What is delicious? Tasty. But tasty doesn't mean good necessarily. Candy is tasty until it means getting a cavity filled; french fries are tasty until it means a heart attack; sushi is tasty, until it means *trichinosis*. We do not want to be separated from God, but we choose something seemingly better. We choose the *created* over the *Creator*. There was a time though, you know, when sin was not. In fact, we didn't even know we *could* sin. All was right in the world so to speak. We had everything we needed. Need was the important thing, but we had not yet discovered "want." Want is different from need. Want is a result of original sin; the original sin of the angels who were banished into a grotesque ugliness called hell. Want is the grasping for something we were never meant to have. If we were meant to have it, then it wouldn't be want; it would be need. And our *Needs* are met.

So we never knew what it was to want in the beginning. We had everything we needed. We could've gone on like that forever; we would've gone on like that forever, unless someone or something introduced "want" to us. It's so fascinating to me that some of the poorest people I've met, don't know they're poor. And then Mother Theresa came out with this quote which I think sums it up. "The rich are not those who have everything; the rich are those who need nothing." To need nothing. That was the state of things. Adam and Eve had it all. They needed nothing. But then another had to intervene and introduce "want." The desire within us that can never be satisfied because it was never meant to be there. He introduced *want* to the woman; who introduced *want* or desire to the man; and it has been there ever since. A baby doesn't cry for want…but for need. Until that child is introduced to "have" and then it "wants." Such was the case for these new creatures. Bliss was not enough. Desire for more drives

173

many through life and yet possession never satisfies that hunger but only aggravates it.

Want focuses on what one does not possess. Desire focuses on what one lacks. Both of these drive us to cling to that which we have no right to possess. How do we know this? Because once we possess it; that which fills not a need; we crave something else. Such was the case when the *diabolos* entered the garden. He would enter the garden again in the first century to try and tempt the one who was present at his very inception. Sin is a moment of "temporary insanity"; but a moment that has repercussions throughout time and space and beyond. We observe the blackness and cold ugliness that was a result of one sin of pride among divine beings. Now witness millions of voices crying out in absolute solitude and misery and you have heard the effect of sin on God. That we repeat a million times a minute the sin of those original creatures before God their maker. The original sin of the desire to be Him. The tears of God are made up of the sins of His creatures in their moments of insanity.

In the Beginning, some of the angels accepted the will of God as their own; others rebelled. Those that rebelled were stripped of the light, the goodness and the beauty. Adam and Eve were stripped of the knowledge of God; of their innocence and of the flawless beauty that comes from dependence on another for everything. The beauty that does not know sickness or labor or death. And so like the demons which fled from the light, Adam and Eve hid in the woods which once gave them food. But unlike those who fled in their ugliness, God sought the humans. This must have enraged the angels who once were so close to the Creator. It gave them a higher resolve that the humans should be relegated to the depths; the only world they knew.

Two questions are asked by God to Adam and Eve. "Where are you?" They respond, "We heard you, but we were naked and ashamed, so we hid." Then God says: "Who told you, you were naked? Who told you to be ashamed? I made your body, did I not? Who told you that you were ugly, unloved and unlovable. Who told you that I had withdrawn from you?" Then we will come to realize, that it was not God who withdrew from us, but we who withdrew from him. Someone…some "it" introduced "want" into the world. And so the question He asks is indeed the right question: "Where are you?"

Try to remember a time in your life (and I pray you can recall such a moment) when you were close to God. When you were devout in prayer and felt as though His presence was always with you. How great that was…what that was like. And yet, somehow, we fell away from that intimacy we shared. How does it happen? I believe that in a world where we are constantly trying to live up to the person people will like, we begin to think God is another we have to live up to, and so who needs it? Just another person with expectations of me. That voice is the voice of the evil one. In scripture the devil is called by two names. The first is *diabolos*, which means the tempter. The second, *satan*, means "the accuser." The latter is often more deadly than the former. The *accuser* is the voice you hear saying, "You are worthless and unworthy of God; you are unlovable and ugly, and useless, and unable to do anything right." That is the voice of the *accuser*. So who do we listen to?

Paul in his letter to the Ephesians says twice, "You were chosen." We are destined to be with God. Called to do something that no one before us could ever do, and no one after us will ever be able to do. But we can't believe that we, in our weakness are worthy, and so we hide. We get so far away from God that He becomes just the "old man in the clouds" the "disinterested spectator" who orbits the world, not caring enough to intervene. He becomes for us no more than a myth, who looks on us suffering down below and does nothing. And yet sometimes, it is only through our suffering that we see His face, perhaps for the first time in our life.

As I was going from high school into college, I thought that I might become a priest (go figure). And so as a result, sex, drugs, alcohol were non issues for me. Don't get me wrong, it was not some kind of moral integrity at that point, or lofty standards that kept me from it… it was simply the thought that I might become a priest. That is the only thing that saved me. But nonetheless, when you cut those things out of your

175

life and you're doing what you think you're supposed to, you can fall into a sin that is far greater than those three. This is the sin I suffered from for a number of years. The sin is pride…the original sin from the beginning of time. And that sin manifested itself most often through condemnation.

Don't get this mixed up with judgement; we are called to judge right from wrong. But condemnation is reducing the person to the thing they do wrong and damning them for it. It is one of the worst sins and the results were catastrophic. I began to isolate myself because no one was good enough. That one was "a drunk"; another "slept around"; still another was a "druggie," and I was too good for that. So more and more I began to turn in on myself, and what resulted was absolute solitude, and depression. For we who are called out of ourselves to love others, I was essentially living in hell. My depression lasted for about two years, during which time I often prayed for death. I still prayed mind you…I never stopped praying. I would ask the Lord to take me because I could never live through this.

Then one evening (while I was praying for such death) the phone rang and it was a friend from across campus. She was sick and wanted to go to the health center, it was midnight. So begrudgingly I agreed to walk her over. She went in to see the doctor and I sat down and opened up a Readers Digest. I opened up to "Quotable Quotes" and saw this quote from a Louis l'Amore novel. And my life was changed forever. I looked around to make sure no one was watching, and tore the page out. And up to a few months ago, still had it framed in my office. I recently gave it to someone who needed it more than I, and she said she would return it when she no longer needed it. That night, the Lord introduced me to love without expectation.

What does *that* mean? It means that I love you whether you love me or not; regardless of what you say or do. That I could never condemn anyone again, because we are all in the same boat. All those people….there but for the grace of God go I. I could have been in any of those situations. And what if that habit was the worst thing they did? They are far better than I. Now don't misunderstand. We are supposed to have expectations of people for high morals; to try hard at academics, sports, etc. Those are expectations that benefit them. I'm talking about a love without expectations that will benefit ME. Love without expectation means I love them simply for their own sake. That if we believe love is self gift, then this is giving a gift without any strings attached.

Do you know how freeing that *IS*? When we can love without expectation we do not need to promote ourselves, we are not insecure, we do not allow the moods of others to determine what ours will be. We have what we NEED, so we do not WANT.

Think of the people in your life now. Some of those you meet in the hall or out in the lot, and they are the people who always want something from you. And you think: "Oh man, what do they need now...what do they want now?" and you avoid them. What about those people who will do anything for you, or give you anything and never ask for return? They are magnets! Because we can see in them a glimmer of God. That is what we are called to be! That is a love that allowed a young girl to say yes to say yes to our Lord when He approached her to be His mother; not knowing the future; the turmoil, responsibility and suffering. To love without expectation is a resounding yes. God said to her: "Where are you?" She answered, "Here I am, I come to do your will." God asks us, "Where are YOU?" What will we say?

Advent is the perfect time to make this happen. You might be thinking: "It's too late. I've already messed up relationships; I'm already too far from God." Adam and Eve felt much the same way. They hid themselves because they saw themselves separated from the Creator. What a grotesque scene that is...so obscene is it to be separated that we run for darkness to hide the obvious. I thought that too; and yet in the mercy of God, He saw fit to give me a miracle. A kindness I begrudgingly did for someone which would change my life forever. God reached out for me, and that's why the one quote changed my life. And this is what it said: "There will come a time in your life when you believe everything is finished...that will be the beginning."

As the serpent watched Adam and Eve leave the garden he considered why is it that these mere creatures all of a sudden are still loved by the Almighty. Certainly this was not fair. But as the Evil one watched, he saw that from that point on, although loved, that the humans were no longer in God's graces. He rejoiced as these favorites of the Almighty were exiled into labor and sickness and even death. The unrest they must have felt as they were told they would "die." What did "die" mean?[65] And so there was still a victory for the Evil one…he still triumphed. There was no possibility that these creatures could ever be with God again….unless…..but no, that would not be possible; would not be practical; would not be…unless…God were selfless.

But that doesn't make sense. One who created it all; why possibly waste the time and effort? Why make the sacrifice? With ultimate power and beauty and goodness… why not just re-create? Why not create beings without free will? Because goodness, beauty….light seek only love. CS Lewis says: "To love at all is to be vulnerable. Love anything, and your heart will certainly be wrung and possibly broken. To keep it safe wrap it carefully round with hobbies and little luxuries; avoid all entanglements. Lock it up safe in the casket or coffin of our selfishness. But in that casket---safe and dark, motionless airless---it will change. It will not be broken; it will become unbreakable, impenetrable, irredeemable. The only place outside of heaven where you can be perfectly safe from all the dangers and perturbations of love is hell."[66]

Love necessitates risk. And this is a risk worth taking. Is it not?

---

65 Pope John Paul II, *The Theology of the Body: Human Love in the Divine Plan*, (Boston: Paulist Press, 1997), 41.

66 C.S. Lewis, *The Four Loves*, (New York: Harcourt, Brace and Company, 1960), 169.

APPENDIX IV
MEDITATION ON HELL

We have sanitized our language and our minds so that nothing that offends our sense of self, our sense of freedom will dare to contaminate our utopian idea. And yet we know in our lives that there are many things beyond our control that creep their ugly reality into our surrealism. One of these things is the least talked about anymore, and yet the most threatening reality to our panacea. Hell. One of the Ignatian exercises is a meditation on hell. One can become so efficient at meditation that it becomes very real. For me, this was the case.

We hear from theologians and some priests that hell does not exist. That a truly loving God would never...could never relegate any soul to the gates of hell. Truly this God who has made an eternal investment by creating a soul would not want to see it destroyed in the abyss we call hell. Therein is the fatal irony. The soul is not destroyed in hell, but the soul wishes it were. The soul lives on into eternity, and the God who created it as an eternal investment, unlike any other must still contemplate that soul every moment of every day of every year for the rest of eternity. If God could be in hell, this is it for Him. What about the soul there?

In my meditation, I heard the shrill cry of someone as if they were being tortured alive. The cry we pray never to hear; the cry of our loved ones perhaps; perhaps someone we don't even know and yet the cry is so loud and painful that we just want it to stop; we will do anything we can to stop it. The gasps of crying so loud; and wailing so continuous that you wonder if they had but a breath. The fatal truth is, they need not breath anymore; and their pain is not physical but spiritual. They are without the one thing that was necessary. Like a terminal cancer that cannot be cured; and cannot kill you; it simply eats you alive again and again and again. But the cancer began to feed long before hell became their eternity.

We would do anything to keep our loved ones from experiencing that type of pain; to keep ourselves from experiencing that type of torture…or would we? We are not asked to fast for years on end; to offer out body as a sacrifice; to wound ourselves or go through some type of mutilating ritual. We are not asked to pray twenty-four hours a day in sorrow for our sins, or to offer continuous oblations to our God. What are we asked to do? "Love God with all your heart mind soul and strength; and love your neighbor as yourself" (Luke 10:27). That is what is required. "But can you drink the cup that I will drink?" (Mark 10:38b)

Can you drink the cup…

That IS the question isn't it. I was contemplating this just the other night. Would I die for my faith? I'm there trying to get out of the thorns in the woods; deer ticks crawling up my legs and arms; blood trailing from me and ready to offer everything I own just to get out of this situation. But is this so unlike how many of us deal with adversity? We are ready to do what it takes to make it go away, or to bring things back to normal. Would I die for Christ, that is the question. As I meditate on it, I want to say yes with all of my being and yet as I'm trying to do this…do this authentically and honestly, I stutter. As I continue to reflect the question is not so much anymore, "Can I die for Christ" as much as it is, "Why do I stutter?" Have I not devoted my life to Christ? Am I not a priest for Christ and yet I actually have to contemplate for a moment (longer than a moment) whether or not I would be willing to die for him?

There are people in other parts of the world who are dying for him daily, many of whom don't have the choice. They are not interrogated as in the first centuries of the Church, nor are they bargained with, in order to save their lives. They are marked as Christians whether they practice the faith or not and are slaughtered. These people dying for their faith, and yet I stutter. My life is not necessarily in jeopardy for practicing Catholicism let alone being a priest in the Latin Church. Why would I hesitate?

And the answer comes very clearly. "Be careful if you are seeking answers, because without a doubt they will be given." I hesitate to embrace the "big death" because I know my weakness with the little deaths I experience every day. And as I take inventory of the little deaths I fail to embrace, the words of Christ echo once again: "Can you drink of the cup of which I drink?" And I want to shout, "YES Lord, I will follow you to your very death." And then he looks at me...peers through me with his omniscient eyes and says: "I don't wish for you to physically die for me; that's too easy." Then I ask, "What is it that you want then Lord?" And He replies: "The one thing you continue to withhold from me...that's all."

"To drink the cup of which I drink does not mean that you must give up your existence. It means can you endure that annoying person who always catches you at the time you least need someone to bother you; it means sitting in class and learning all you need to learn so that you can provide for my people; it means taking care of those who need you even though they can never possibly pay you back; it means giving without any expectation of return and it means praying when people won't see you; celebrating Mass as though it is your first, your last, your only Mass. It means struggling with the many temptations without becoming cynical; and it means loving your brothers and sisters, even when it's difficult. THAT is drinking the cup of which I drink."

I know why I stutter now. These are the little deaths that prepare me for the ultimate one. And yet I have not handled them nearly as well as an apostle should...as a disciple should. "To drink the cup" means to embrace the little deaths, and then each of these will prepare us for the ultimate one. So that when that one comes (as a thief in the night) we will not be shocked as one who is afraid of the unknown...we will be surprised as one feels at the age of three on Christmas day.

APPENDIX VI
SQUIRRELS AND CROWS:
A KINGDOM DIVIDED AMONG ITSELF CANNOT ENDURE.
ORIGINAL FABLE BASED ON MY EXPERIENCES WITH THE CRITTERS SURROUNDING THE CHURCH AND RECTORY AT GOOD SHEPHERD CHURCH OF

She was on the cross. There were "stickies" on either end, but she was small enough to avoid being hurt. Schwartza was just learning how to fly, and did not quite grasp the way her tail was supposed to work with her wings to guide her along. But that didn't matter to her. To fly...that was the ultimate adventure. Then she spied him. That gray rat down on the ground trying to carry the seed up the tree. Those awful grays, she thought. The world would have been better without them.

You see, the crows and the squirrels (grays) were at war. Only the older crows, with gray now frosting their feathers remembered the beginning of the war. The grays who were there at the time were now gone. How often does it happen that we become so involved in fighting each other, that after awhile we forget what we were fighting about. It appeared that the crows and the squirrels would remain bitter enemies. For anything to change it would take a miracle.

Schwartza continued to enjoy the cool breeze sweeping over the roof of the church, and rising just enough to give her a gentle lift. She watched as the resident human scurried across the stone ground towards her. Her gaze then fixed once again on the gray. The squirrel she was watching had only a worm-like tail, for all the fluffy fur was gone. He was soon joined by another with an ashen tint to his head and back.

"Pyre," said the squirrel with the wormy tail. "Help me get this corny thing up the tree! The sky looks like it's gonna start *watering* and I want to make sure this is stored." Pyre looked doubtful. "So

182

you want to get *that nut* up there? What are you gonna do with it once it's stored?" "I'm gonna eat it," said the wormy tailed squirrel. Pyre said: "Then why don't you just eat it now, and save the energy of storing it?" Pyre didn't yet understand the job of planning for the winter. "Never mind, I'll just...." But the wormy- tailed squirrel was cut off, as a dark shadow passed over them. Pyre was frozen with fear, and couldn't speak, while the wormy-tailed squirrel began digging a hole. Just as suddenly as the shadow had appeared, it vanished. "Wa whaa was that?" asked Pyre. The other squirrel just looked at her and sighed... "Let's get up the tree before it returns."

Pyre and the other gray were siblings, but to different litters. See, squirrels give birth to three or four babies a season. Pyre was born just this spring along with two others. These two traveled everywhere together and were often seen playing tag, up and down the tree. The resident human had named them Podo and Kodo after two ferrets he saw in a film once. So it was Podo, Kodo, and Pyre. The other siblings were also three in number, but were a year older. There was the one with the wormy-tail; the one who never seemed to be on the ground, but jumped from tree to tree, named Ptera; and finally the one with a rusty red patch on his head and back. The resident human named him Pentecost. The squirrels spent their days playing and storing nuts and making nests...and warring with the crows. Not even the grays' parents recalled why there was such a problem among the crows and the squirrels, but they knew to keep their babies inside. For one gray swears the war began when a flock of crows attacked and killed a gray, only to eat it in front of its family.

The crows knew differently. They typically traveled in gangs, which created part of their status as unlikable creatures. They made these awful "caws" in the morning and at night; when standing in territory or flying away. This was enough to want them gone, but the fact that the squirrels had heard the legends about the killing made them want to destroy the crows all together. Often if the grays found eggs of the crows they would drop them from the nest. Other times if they found a nest was being built, they would destroy it just as fast as the crow could build it. There seemed no way that the two would ever be able to get along.

Schwartza was enjoying the sun on her face, and then suddenly, something changed. A dark shadow blotted out the sun, and a chill ran through her body. She couldn't move; she was frozen. She waited and heard nothing…she looked straight ahead, and saw nothing. And then she felt the cross on which she was standing move slightly, as though some weight had been added to the other side. Out of the corner of her eye, she peered around the top of the cross, trying not to be noticed, and the worst of her nightmares came true…it was him!

The grays had been meeting more often as of late. Most of the time when winter was approaching, or there was a drought or something that affected the whole community, they would meet to discuss stuff. But meetings every other day…that was a lot. "But they almost took him this time," said one of the grays surrounded by her children. "It wasn't even close mom" responded the wormy-tailed squirrel. He recalled the day he was outside of the human's nest (the one who named them). He was fiddling around with another nut, looking towards winter. At one point he recalled looking up at the clear wall of the human's nest and seeing him act peculiar. "He was opening his mouth and making motions like he was being attacked, but I could hear nothing. I remember feeling a chill, and just as I turned I spotted it. Dropping down off of the large metal tree with the fire box at the top. The human resident called it the *Sentinel* (whatever that means). It dropped from the box, but was much faster than the crows, not even flapping it wings. I was frozen, and my gaze was fixed on that crazy human dancing around inside his nest like he was trying to run. RUN! That's what filled my mind and I did it. I ran to the nearest tree, and he was quickly closing in on me. All I could think about was all those nuts I'd stored…that got me runnin' faster. I ran so fast, that when I got to the tree I couldn't stop and ran head first into it. I shook it off, and saw that his claws were almost in my back. I darted up the tree like Podo and Kodo do every day, and made myself flat like a leaf (like mamma taught us). The *Sentinel* darted away in anger, I could see fire from his nostrils (well not really, but a good effect) and then just hovered like one of those giant metal hummingbirds the humans have. And then he smiled, as though he would see me again. Whew! Well…maybe it *was* close."

Meanwhile, one of the ancient crows cawed to the others. They all surrounded one of their own. Another ancient one, with gray trim lay dead on the ground, three puncture wounds in the chest. "This was done by no squirrel," said the elder. "Three wounds on the top and one large on the bottom. This is the work of a *Buteo*. Their eyes were downcast on their fallen companion, as a shadow darkened the scene, and the *Sentinel's* eyes saw its prey. Immediately, the ancient crow took to flight in the direction of the shadow, and the other crows followed, cawing loudly and flying wildly. The ancient one reached the *Buteo* in mid air first, and reached for its eyes, but alone he could do nothing. With one sweep from its large wing, the crow was knocked out of sorts, and by the time the others had reached the hawk he was well out of range. They all charged their falling comrade, who regained his senses before hitting the ground. They ate what was left of the dead crow, (for that's what crows eat) and they flew off to plan their next move. Podo and Kodo were watching the whole seen; even when they ate their own.

Schwartza began to tremble. Why had she ever come out alone, barely able to fly and so young. She was scared to death and her feet were frozen. What could she do? If she tried to fly, the *Buteo* would simply pick her out of the air and gobble her up. She had heard the stories the elders told about one of the ancient ones. She thought about letting out a caw, certainly the others would hear her and come to her rescue, but when she tried to, nothing came out. She was stuck. And then she felt the cross move slightly and realized what it was…the *Buteo* was slowing inching his way toward her.

Ptera was so glad the meeting was over. "Those gatherings were all about *grown-nut* talk and nothing fun." These latest meetings were pretty scary too. About this *Sentinel* who terrorizes the grays and the crows. They had heard one of the crows had been eaten whole, while in mid air. They heard that the *Sentinel* breathes fire and has claws like

185

the "stickies" on gutters and rooftops. "Glad I don't have to worry, I rarely go on the ground" said Ptera, and that was true. She had this amazing skill to jump from tree to tree to roof to tree, never touching the ground. One of the elder grays told her that the name *Ptera* means "wing." Ptera was hopping from tree to tree, hoping to be getting back to the nest for some eats, and as she jumped on the roof of the human's nest, she leaped over the top to the other side and ran straight into something fluffy. She thought it was a crow but then she saw who it was. It let out a scream, the worse sound she had ever heard, and just then Pentecost jumped on the roof and started barking. Who'd a thought grays could bark? The *Sentinel* ignored him, and just then a giant crow with gray around his beak landed on the roof in front of Ptera. The crow was shaking, but did not move. The *Sentinel* lunged toward him with talons extended just as Pentecost jumped at the hawk. Ptera slid down the roof, and the *Sentinel*, now disoriented took off, hovered and then flew beyond sight. Pentecost, now facing the ancient crow flipped back on the tree and made himself flat. "Wait!" said the crow. And neither of them moved.

The young fledgling crow cowered now on the metal cross. The *Buteo* moved slowly to the left, moving only its feet. She looked at the spear heads, cruelly curved off of the yellow toes and the rusty red feathers below them that formed a tail. She finally decided that if she was going to live, she must act. Very slowly she opened her left foot, which was barely big enough to clasp the metal cross, and slid it away from the *Sentinel*. She knew that she would easily disappear in one of its talons, but could not allow the fear to overcome her. She was still trembling, and even more so now...because for the first time, the *Sentinel* turned its head and looked straight at its prey. Schwartza pretended not to see, but just slid her other foot to meet the other.

The crow was old and wise and spoke to the gray. "What is it that you eat as grays?" he asked. "What is it to you?" he replied. Pentecost was still weary of the crow, having been raised on stories of the nasty things crows did. "What is it you eat?" asked the crow a second time. "We eat the fruits from the trees, like the corny nuts." "What would happen if you didn't eat the fruit; if you allowed it to go untouched?"

asked the crow. "It would eventually become another tree I suppose. That happens sometimes when we don't dig'em up after the winter." "Do you think these trees are alive?" "Most definitely" said Pentecost, "they eat just as we do, and provide homes for us grays." "Then why do you eat their children my dear gray?" "What are you saying?" yelled Pentecost. He was becoming angry. "You told me, young gray, that you eat the fruit of the tree. If left alone, that fruit becomes a tree, and therefore it must be the offspring of the very tree…the one you said *IS* living. Are you then a killer of young trees gray?" Pentecost was struck. He didn't know what to say. "Of course not!" said the crow. "You are no more a killer of young trees than we are killers of grays. Just as you feed on the fruit, which otherwise would rot, we crows feed on those things which have died. We aren't killers, we are scavengers. We eat the dead. Imagine if all the animals killed were never eaten. Imagine if the bodies just stacked up and rotted." Pentecost thought about this and then replied: "You killed a gray and were caught eating it." The crow let out a sigh and responded: "The gray was killed by a human machine. We chose not to allow the body to rot, but to feed. Even when you saw us eat our own, young gray (and I know you were watching) we did him honor, for now he, is part of *us*. But now my little gray we have a shadow in our midst who alone can end our lives as we know it. It is *a dark shadow* over us and our young, both grays and caws, and no one is safe as long as it is with us. Speak with your kin, and I will with mine…history will not serve us, if it threatens to steal our future."

The little crow was now at the very edge of the cross, right next to the "stickie". The *Buteo* did not hide his desire at this point and now made bigger strides toward the little caw. He crouched down close to the cross as he looked on Schwartza, and a smile formed across his hooked-spike beak. She decided that if this were her last moment, she would at least let out a caw and take to flight. All her muscles tightened as she braced for the worst. She crouched her tiny body toward the metal of the cross, tensed her legs and then….WHOOSH!…she froze and looking over saw the hawk lose balance a bit and then just as suddenly, WOEWSH! From the front of him a black blur flew down and just brushed his head, knocking it back a bit. And then another Wheewsh!

From the side. Each time, Schwartza crouched a little toward the metal support on which she was standing and then she looked up and there must have been fifty caws, cawing out and diving at the hawk. Then, for the first time she looked into its eyes, and saw something she never expected…fear.

The hawk lunged for her, but as it did, one of the ancient ones (the one who spoke with Pentecost) dove between them and clawed at the hawk, and for a moment they were both tangled talons in mid air. The hawk let go and the ancient one tumbled, landing in a tree top. The *Sentinel* swooped down to the ground, where he was seemingly safe from the crows. Just then the worm-tailed gray and Pyre jumped over at him and started doing flips and chasing their tails while jumping at the *Sentinel*. The *Sentinel* leapt at them, but was confused, because shortly after, Pentecost came in as well. The hawk leapt up to a branch, and there were Podo and Kodo running around him, jumping on branches, and shaking down the acorns from the branch above. The *Sentinel* began inching toward them, ready to at least finish one gray today, and then SWOOP! Ptera came flying down from the branches and make a grab for the branch above the hawk's head, but misjudged the distance, and tackled the bird. The hawk let out a painful scream as Ptera was once again eye to eye with the predator. They both hit the ground, but Ptera having been cushioned by the feathers, jumped up and ran. Immediately all the squirrels surrounded the hawk and began jumping around. The hawk scrambled to its feet and took to flight, only to be surrounded by the crows. They began dive bombing the hawk and side scratching with their talons. They followed him off into the distance, attacking mercilessly until the hawk could be seen no more. The crows return with a victorious caw, while the squirrels let out barks of joy.

The crows took to the trees surrounding the squirrels and the squirrels grouped into a circle, ready for anything. Nobody moved. What was to happen now? Bitter enemies for so long and now a standoff. Pentecost crawled forward toward the front of the circles where the crows were gathered in the tree. And there lay the ancient one in the grass. He sat up, a scratch across his eye and his wing folded in an unnatural bend...and he smiled. Schwartza clumsily flew down to where the ancient one lay. Pentecost bowed to the crow, Schwartza put her head under her wing, and the ancient crow in turn put his head under his wing. The crows flew off, cawing victoriously, while the ancient one walked in that direction with the life he had saved. The war between the grays and caws was no more.

In fact to this day, neither recalls what they had fought over for so many years...but not a single creature will ever forget the day an alliance was formed that was able to overcome the enemy. It's amazing what can happen when we focus on the true enemy, instead of each other.

Bibliography
of Major Published Works

Bellarmine, Saint Robert "Treatise on the Ascent of the Mind to God", in *The Liturgy of the Hours: According to the Roman Rite*. volume IV. New York: Catholic Book Publishing Co., 1975.

Benedict XVI. *Deus Caritas Est*. Encyclical Letter. Vatican City: Libreria Editrice Vaticana, 2006.

Bishops' Committee on Marriage and Family. *Always Our Children: A Pastoral Message to Parents of Homosexual Children and Suggestions for Pastoral Ministers.*

van Breeman, Peter G., SJ. *Called by Name*. Denville, NJ: Dimension Books, 1976.

_____. *The God Who Won't Let Go*. Notre Dame, IN: Ave Maria Press, 1991.

DeMello, Anthony SJ. *The Way to Love: The Last Meditations of Anthony De Mello*. New York: Doubleday Press, 1991.

_____. *Awareness: The Perils and Opportunities of Reality*. New York: Doubleday, 1992.

Frankl, Viktor E. *Man's Search for Meaning*. 3rd ed. New York: Simon and Schuster, 1984.

Groeshel, Benedict CFR. *Arise from Darkness: What to Do When Life Doesn't Make Sense*. San Francisco, CA: Ignatius Press, 1995.

John Paul II. *The Theology of the Body: Human Love in the Divine Plan*. Boston: Paulist Press, 1997.

Keller, Phillip. *Shepherd looks at Psalm 23*. Grand Rapids, Michigan, 1970.

Kollar, Charles Allen. *Solution-Focused Pastoral Counseling: An Effective Short- Term Approach for Getting People Back on Track*. Grand Rapids, Michigan: Zondervan, 1997.

L'Amore, Louis: *Lonely on the Mountain*. Bantam books, 1984.

Landry, Roger J. *A homily delivered at Espirito Santo Parish*, Fall River MA, Reprinted by the Catholic Educator's Resource Center, February 3, 2002.

Levinas, Emmanuel. *Otherwise than Being or Beyond Essence*. trans. Alphonso Lingis. The Hague: Nijhoff, 1981.

Lewis, C.S. *The Four Loves*. New York: Harcourt, Brace and Company, 1960.

_____. *Mere Christianity*. San Francisco, CA: Harper Collins Publishers, 1980.

Lucado, Max . *Just Like Jesus*. Nashville TN: Word Publishing, 1998.

Madrid, Patrick. *Search and Rescue: How to bring your Family and Friends into- or Back into – The Catholic Church*. Manchester, NH: Sophia Institute Press, 2001.

Plato. *Republic: Book VII*, page 186-188, transl. By G.M.A. Grube. Cambridge: Hackett Publishing Company, Inc., 1992.

Rolheiser, Ronald OMI. *The Holy Longing: The Search for a Christian Spirituality*. New York: Doubleday, 1999.

_____. *Against the Infinite Horizon: The Finger of God in Our Everyday Lives*. New York: The Crossroad Publishing Company, 2001.

_____. *The Shattered Lantern: Rediscovering a Felt Presence of God.* New York: The Crossroad Publishing Company, 2001.

Saving Jane. "You Say" from *Girl Next Door.* Umvd, Labels, 2006.

Shea, John. *Eating with the Bridegroom: The Spiritual Wisdom of the Gospels for Christian Preachers and Teachers.* Collegeville, MN: Liturgical Press, 2004.

Sheen, Fulton J. *The World's First Love.* New York, NY: McGraw-Hill Co., 1952.

_____. *Lift Up Your Hearts.* New York: McGraw-Hill Book Company, Inc., 1950.

_____. *Preface to Religion* in *The Angel's Blackboard: The Best of Fulton J. Sheen.* Liguori, Missori: Liguori/Triumph Press, 1995.

Tonne, Arthur. *5-Minute Homilies on the Gospels of Cycles A, B, C.* Green Bay, Wisconsin: Alt Publishing Co., 1977.

ABOUT THE AUTHOR

Fr. Michael Rothan was ordained a priest for the Roman Catholic Diocese of Harrisburg, PA in 2004. He was formerly a scientist and teacher, receiving his B.S. in Biology from Shippensburg University and teacher certification from Millersville University. He began his studies for the priesthood at St. Vincent Seminary in Latrobe, PA where he received his B.A. in Philosophy; an M.A. in Sacred Scripture, and a Master of Divinity Degree. He is currently the Pastor of St. Benedict the Abbot Church in Lebanon PA and Chaplain at Lebanon Catholic. This is his first book.

Printed in the United States
208289BV00006B/42/P